LESSONS
FROM
NORTH
CAROLINA

★ ★ ★

LESSONS FROM NORTH CAROLINA

RACE, RELIGION, TRIBE, AND THE FUTURE OF AMERICA

Gene Nichol

— BLAIR —

Printed in the United States of America
Cover design by Callie Riek & Miranda Young
Interior design by April Leidig

Blair is an imprint of Carolina Wren Press.

BLAIR

*The mission of Blair/Carolina Wren Press is to seek out, nurture,
and promote literary work by new and underrepresented writers.*

We gratefully acknowledge the ongoing support of general operations by the
Durham Arts Council's United Arts Fund and the North Carolina Arts Council.

Library of Congress Cataloging-in-Publication Data
Names: Nichol, Gene R., 1951– author.
Title: Lessons from North Carolina : race, religion, tribe, and the future
of America / Gene Nichol.
Description: Durham : Blair, 2023. | Includes bibliographical references.
Identifiers: LCCN 2022053402 (print) | LCCN 2022053403 (ebook) |
ISBN 9781958888018 (paperback) | ISBN 9781958888025 (ebook)
Subjects: LCSH: Political culture—North Carolina. | Political participation—North
Carolina. | Identity politics—North Carolina. | Right and left (Political science)—
North Carolina. | North Carolina—Politics and government—21st century.
Classification: LCC JK4189 .N54 2023 (print) | LCC JK4189 (ebook) |
DDC 306.209756—dc23/eng/20221206
LC record available at https://lccn.loc.gov/2022053402
LC ebook record available at https://lccn.loc.gov/2022053403

CONTENTS

LESSONS
FROM
NORTH
CAROLINA

have thought much of North Carolina. I wouldn't claim to understand it. That's the work of lifetimes, maybe many of them. But I have come to know that North Carolina is my place—after many years, many tries. It's my home, the place that I love. Even when it seems not to love me—or perhaps that's too grandiose—even when it seems not to love people like me or people whom I seem to be like. I'm all in. Its mountains, its small towns, its rivers and streams, its barbecue, its basketball (growing up as a Texas football player, I never dreamed there could be a higher cause), its cool cities (like Durham and Asheville), its battles, its challenges, its histories, its cruelties, its informalities, its habitually opened door, its heroism, and its eternal refusal to surrender . . .

It's my place. Not Texas, where I'm from originally, whose exaggerated, defining machoism is both comical and cruel but mainly fake. (I grew up there when everybody didn't wear cowboy hats, like all the imported Yankees there do now.) And not Virginia, whose fawning embrace of its past, stifling and self-deluding classism, and noblesse oblige, which turns out to carry neither nobility nor obligation but only pretense and privilege, is the opposite of uplifting. Nor even Colorado, which inspires and triggers much-justified awe. But Colorado is nature, not society. And I figured out halfway through my life that I'm (surprisingly) still a southerner—even deeply so, for good and ill. That means, too, that for me, North Carolina is a more potent illustration of the challenges and meaning of America than even Colorado, with its hopes and horizons.

I say all this without knowing or even much wondering whether North Carolina is the most pointed battleground over the soul and meaning of the United States and the American promise. Maybe that's actually Georgia, or Texas or Arizona, or Florida or Wisconsin (though I can't for the life of me figure out what all those right-wing Wisconsin folks have to be so pissed about). And for me, to be candid, North Carolina is mostly about its people. It's Bill Friday, Bill Aycock, and Bill Finlator. It's Frank Graham, Terry Sanford, Dan Pollitt, Tom Lambeth, and Julius Chambers; it's Ella Baker, Pauli Murray, Shirley Edwards, and Rosanell Eaton; it's Dean Smith, Bill Guthridge, John Hope Franklin, Doris Betts, Dick Richardson, William Barber, Irv Joyner, Roz Pelles, Tim Tyson, Bill Ferris, and Pat Devine. It's other people you perhaps wouldn't know but whom I worship. It's the native home of my wife and her parents and the chosen home of my kids. It's been a short love affair for me, only twenty years, but it's been a deep and lasting one. And regardless of what happens, it abides.

This book is largely about matters that I wouldn't have anticipated when I moved to Chapel Hill in 1999. I had come to the University of North Carolina after a long stint as dean of the law school at the University of Colorado. I was enthusiastic about UNC for two reasons.

First, for a lot of us southerners by blood, the state of North Carolina had long been regarded as a leading edge—perhaps the leading edge—of progressivism in the American South. To be sure, Carolina's progressive habits were often timid and halting, and usually exceedingly modest. Still, the Tar Heel State was decidedly not to be confused with Mississippi, Alabama, South Carolina, or Georgia.

Second, I have a thing for the University of North Carolina itself. Quite intentionally, I've spent my entire academic career—as a student, a professor, a dean, and a president—at public universities. Don't get me wrong; I have nothing against private colleges. But it has always seemed to me that the crucial democratizing work of higher education in the United States is played out, almost fully, in our great and ambitious state institutions. And though they have their challenges, the mission of public higher education is a near-perfect one: to bring the illumination and opportunity that are offered by the lamp of learning to all—rich and poor, high and low, rural and urban, newly arrived and anciently pedigreed, all races, all genders, and all sexualities. All can, the theory goes, deploy education's prospects to make the promises of egalitarian democracy real. I'm a believer.

And also, for me, the University of North Carolina was the country's greatest public university—or at least the greatest state university that actually wanted to be a public university. Michigan and Virginia are terrific universities, to be sure, but they have long since enthusiastically cast aside their public missions in order to emulate the fanciest private universities. Berkeley didn't yearn, existentially, to be private, but perennial California state-budget crises effectively forced privatization upon it. UNC, on the other hand, was decidedly public and proud to be so. It didn't hurt that my wife was a Carolina undergraduate, so I'd been hearing Tar Heel tales for years. For me, UNC was the tall cotton. It still is.

But much has changed here in the last two decades. North Carolina's politics are no longer moderate or congenial, nor can they be deemed progressive—even if one believes there is a "southern progressive" government to be found in the land. Since 2011, North Carolina has experienced a powerful Republican revolution. The formerly purported "beacon of southern progress" is now what national pundits call a "laboratory for extremism," a "poster child for regressive, conservative policies."[1] Experts claim that the state has experienced a "bigger and quicker shift to the right than any other state in the union."[2] The *New York Times* has decried the "grotesque damage" that has been done by the new North Carolina Republican majority "to a tradition of caring for the least fortunate."[3] What was once deemed a rare example of "farsightedness in the South"—a singular "exception in a region of poor education, intolerance and tightfistedness"—has "dismantled a reputation that took years to build."[4] North Carolina's state government has become, as the *New York Times* explained, a "demolition derby, tearing down years of progress in public education, tax policy, racial equality in the courtroom and equal access to the electoral system."[5] Others have noted that Carolina's citizens, including a diverse and growing minority population, are being "disenfranchised by the Republican-controlled General Assembly," brazenly dismissing the will of the people and "showing no compunction about curtailing civil liberties."[6] Tellingly, North Carolina Republicans "have continued to pass regressive laws that subvert the Constitution they claim to defend."[7]

The University of North Carolina has been drawn into the fray as well. Over the last decade, the N.C. General Assembly and its appointees on the UNC Board of Governors have become nationally and even internationally notorious for using their political powers to fire presidents and chancellors for partisan purposes, engaging in racially discriminatory hiring and tenure decisions, closing academic centers and programs in violation of free expression and academic freedom, punishing faculty members for engaging in constitutionally protected speech, and demanding leaders who will submit to the ideological requirements of Republican lawmakers and their representatives. National academic reviewing organizations have "resoundingly condemned" the UNC Board of Governors for instituting a "climate of institutional racism," repeatedly "violating standards of academic freedom," and demonstrating "alarming levels of political interference" with North Carolina public universities.[8] These very public wounds are deep and exceedingly difficult to repair. As a result, one of the world's great public universities is severely threatened.[9] Across a spanning social and political landscape, the new North Carolina is not like the old North Carolina.

Like a lot of Tar Heels, I'll admit to being surprised by these developments. Most of us would not have guessed that after all these generations, North Carolina lawmakers would opt to try to repeal the twentieth century. And the idea that they would say to academics, "You work for me, and so you'll say what I tell you to say," seems so, well, Stone Age. The new North Carolina has embraced a vivid and trailblazing war on democracy, equality, and constitutional law. Its crusade against people of color, poor people, LGBTQ+ folks, women, public schools and universities, the environment, and the courts is pioneering. It's also much documented. I've written a previous book about it myself.[10] We're right-wing revolutionaries in North Carolina now, even if a lot of us are shocked to learn it.

Still, I'm even more surprised by the *way* that we have chosen to be revolutionary. When push has come to shove, many of our leaders have determined to put aside much of what we have committed to stand for in order to perpetuate their own group's superiority—in short, placing tribe over democracy and power over constitutive principle. As I'll discuss in these pages, we do it in race, in religion, in partisanship, in poverty, in sexuality, and in heritage—saying, repeatedly, seemingly without embarrassment, that some people count and others don't, or at least that some people count more than others. Some of us are full members, the real tribe, the full Americans, the owners, while others may be allowed to enter or to remain but are viewed more like tenants or passers-through. They exist here at the main folks' sufferance. The real tribe may tolerate them to some extent, but that's the most that can be asked of them. If our creeds or constitutions seem to demand more, to require equal dignity and participation, to require full membership, then those creeds and constitutions—despite all the blood and sweat and sacrifice they have triggered—will simply have to give way. If we have spoken solemnly of democracy and equality, then we didn't *really* mean it—it was mere pretense. It was a charade unless our own permanent ascendancy was understood to be the crucial part of the package. We believe in democracy as long as we win; we believe in equality only if we're allowed to dominate. So it's not only necessary that we beat our adversaries at the ballot box or on the statehouse floor; we need to disqualify them, exclude them, or restrict their participation. Equal justice under law carries this damning, disqualifying asterisk.

Let me try to put it more formally.

In 1935, German American political theorist Carl Friedrich wrote that "to be an American is an ideal, while to be a Frenchman is a fact."[11] Friedrich wasn't out to disparage the French. He meant, rather, that in the United States, national membership is not based on race, religion, language, tribe, geography, pedigree, or ancestry. It is, instead, lodged in an idea, a commitment. It's in what Abraham Lincoln saw as our nation's "primary cause": the principle of "liberty to all."[12]

Lyndon Johnson described the centrality of our creedal promise in his most eloquent speech, introducing the Voting Rights Act: "This was the first nation in the history of the world to be founded with a purpose. The great phrases of that purpose sound in every American heart—'All men are created equal,' government 'by consent of the governed.'"[13] Lincoln named that promise in our most important national document as the foundation of both the nation and the civil war that he was compelled to fight—"that government of the people, by the people, for the people, shall not perish from the earth." Former president Barack Obama put it less philosophically in a recent conversation with Bruce Springsteen: "America is a place where you don't have to look a certain way, it's fealty to a creed that matters."[14] To be an American demands a pledged and devoted notion, not a claim of ancestry or purported privilege.

That means, of course, it is possible to behave in ways that are un-American, in ways that violate the American promise, rejecting the very mission of our nation. It is possible to be guilty of casting aside our constitutive agreement, betraying both our declared meaning and the sustained sacrifice of millions stretched over centuries to make, as Rev. Dr. Martin Luther King Jr. put it, "the promises of democracy real." To my perhaps naive horror, North Carolina Republicans have repeatedly shown themselves willing to discard these commitments in order to ensure their own power. They have broken the compact in order to entrench themselves—defining commitments be damned.

Thus, we have opened a debate about what it means to be an American, what America itself means, and what it assumes. We are not alone in this, of course. The presidency of Donald Trump has forced this conversation in the starkest and most dangerous and humiliating terms.[15] But it does seem to me that we've been in this present-day iteration for a little longer than most of the rest of the nation. For at least a dozen years, folks in North Carolina have faced and endured a war against democracy, equality, and even truth itself. So the battle, then, has frequently collapsed into a fight for human decency itself. As a result, we might have modest lessons and warnings to offer the rest of the country.

I claim no great wisdom on this crucial front—only some modest experience in the shoving match. Not just in these disagreements about who we are, who counts, and how that matters and what it demands of us, but also about some institutions that are meant to aid us in our joint and public prospects—like law, education, and politics. I'm an academic by training and temperament, but life in North Carolina can force a student of democratic constitutionalism to become something of a practitioner as well. A few of those experiences are touched on here.

It has been stunning to see the Republican N.C. General Assembly embrace a campaign of exclusion and marginalization against African American Tar Heels. It seems, simply put, so 1954, or even 1898.[16] Still, as historians remind us, it reflects a pattern that consistently recurs, marking our history every bit as powerfully as our highest aspirations do.[17] And, as the last decade has shown, the rejection of constitutional equality on this central, defining front can be contagious and imperialistic. As safeguards and protections related to race are discarded, they become more easily cast aside on issues of religion, politics, income, sexuality, gender, and deliberative democracy as well, favoring, in each instance, raw power over equal participation, equal opportunity, and equal dignity. Tribe is placed over constitutive principle, ascendancy and historical privilege over the American promise itself. This wounds not only the most vulnerable among us but all of us, our defining and much-sacrificed-for national venture. And as the January 6 coup attempt illustrates, the lust for tribal dominance threatens all that matters—everything.

At the close of his long and remarkable life, Frederick Douglass offered his country straightforward advice rooted in his own blood and sacrifice: "Banish the idea that one class must rule over another. Recognize the fact that the rights of the humblest citizen are as worthy of protection as are those of the highest, and your problem will be solved."[18]

Douglass's prescription, and its implicit warning, haunts and challenges us today. I fear that this democracy will not be saved or righted by the exertions of law or traditional bartering and incrementalist politics. Our national character will be secured only by the courageous and unflagging commitment of engaged, idealistic, and equality-ensuring citizens. We are not only the heirs of freedom, but also, in the end, its guarantors.

CHAPTER ONE

Rejecting the American Promise
The Re-Embrace of Racial Supremacy

There's a tendency in this country for people, particularly in
White America, to escape behind American exceptionalism and not
to actually deal with what is real right in front of our faces.
—LaTosha Brown, Cofounder, Black Voters Matter[1]

ike a lot of folks, I was much surprised and much delighted that Barack
Obama carried North Carolina in 2008. I was also surprised, a couple
of years later, by the resulting political backlash. In 2010, Republicans
took over both houses of the General Assembly by substantial
margins. Then, in 2012, Pat McCrory won the governor's race—securing
Republican control of all three branches of state government for the first
time since 1870. The resulting political vice grip included veto-proof majorities in both chambers. Change came quickly—big time.

Something else, less noticed perhaps, occurred as well. North Carolina became effectively ruled by the all-white Republican caucuses of the
North Carolina General Assembly. As of this writing, the legislative racial
hegemony remains intact. In 2022, there are no Black Republican members in the House or Senate even though North Carolina is almost one-
quarter African American and about four out of ten Tar Heels are people
of color. There are, at present, twenty-nine Black members in the House,
but they're all Democrats. All sixty-five Republican representatives are
white. There are ten Black senators and two Asian American senators—
again, all Democrats. The twenty-nine ruling Senate Republicans are all

white. There were similar racial breakdowns in 2011, 2013, 2015, 2017, and 2019.[2]

So when the Republican caucuses of the North Carolina General Assembly repair to their closed meetings to craft the rules for the state, no person of color rises to object to the ensuing legal mandates because none are in the room. One hundred and fifty-four years after the ratification of the Fourteenth Amendment, North Carolina government is dominated by the all-white Republican caucuses of the General Assembly. And, seemingly, no one is much surprised. No one talks about it. This unstated transgression against the American promise is apparently expected. For us, "liberty and justice for all" seems to come with a notable and mission-defeating qualifier. And we readily allow the pattern to repeat itself.

I don't mean to overstate the singularity of North Carolina on this front. National studies report that fewer than 10 percent of the nearly 7,500 state legislators serving across the country are Black, but astonishingly, only thirteen of those African American lawmakers are Republican—thirteen.[3] A recent Pew study found that in the United States Congress, non-white Senate and House of Representative members are 83 percent Democratic and 17 percent Republican. Only three Republican members of the United States Senate are Black or Latino (Ted Cruz, Marco Rubio, and Tim Scott).[4] So the Tar Heel State is hardly alone in its Republican lawmaking racialization. Still, zero is zero. And it's year after year.

I'll admit that I don't know what North Carolina's Republican lawmakers think of this persistent exclusion—whether they are proud of it, embarrassed by it, or simply unphased by it, psychologically unaware. I can't see into their hearts. I probably haven't tried hard enough.[5] But I do know they put up with it. They engage in white people's government. I wouldn't have thought, in 2022, that anyone would.

To be candid, I don't doubt that at some point in the near or distant future, the North Carolina Republican legislative caucuses will add to their rolls a Black or brown member or two, allowing them to reach the more rhetorically congenial label of "overwhelmingly" or "almost entirely" white groupings—if for no other reason than appearance's sake. But I fear that that won't reflect a rediscovered belief in our defining commitment to successful integration or meaningful opportunity for the entire Tar Heel polity. That's especially true with the cover, often provided by the United States Supreme Court itself, that "we're not out to punish Black people, we just want to punish our (Democratic) adversaries. We can't help that so many African Americans are Democrats."[6] Either way, the party will operate in open disdain for an allegiance to "liberty and justice for all."

And, to be clear, the impact of government by all-white caucuses in North Carolina is not just aesthetic. Since capturing the General Assembly in 2011, Republican lawmakers have delivered a statutory legacy that precisely echoes their racialized membership. In a sentence, they have repeatedly, pervasively, intentionally, and invidiously deployed government power to diminish the electoral, representational, legal, educational, and dignitary rights of African Americans. The Republican caucuses of the North Carolina General Assembly not only appear to be white enclaves; they govern like them.

To (briefly) make the point: Upon achieving a governing majority in 2011, the Republican General Assembly drew new congressional districts to extend and entrench their party's power by violating the electoral rights of African Americans. The federal courts ruled, explicitly, that despite legislative claims to the contrary, the House districts had been designed to limit Black voter effectiveness.[7] The state districts that Republican lawmakers produced to govern their own elections topped even that. They created, another court concluded, one of the "largest racial gerrymanders ever confronted by a federal court," resulting in "a widespread, serious and longstanding constitutional violation."[8] Judges determined that the transgression was so pronounced that it deprived Black North Carolinians of a "constitutionally adequate voice in the state legislature."[9] The deprivation was sufficiently fundamental that "it interfered with the very mechanism by which people confer their sovereignty."[10] I'm a constitutional lawyer by trade. I've been reading judicial opinions for almost fifty years. I've rarely seen a court say anything like that.

Not wanting to rest on their laurels, in 2013, the all-white Republican caucuses enacted a massive voter suppression bill—deemed by election-law scholars to be the most restrictive passed by a state in more than fifty years. The provision introduced a racially slanted voter identification requirement aimed at restricting access to the ballot. It also ended same-day voter registration, shortened the early voting period, eliminated out-of-precinct voting, and restricted various early-registration practices. Still another federal court concluded that Republican leaders had studied every mechanism that elevated Black turnout and then, with "almost surgical precision," eliminated or restricted each practice. All the lawmakers' talk about "ballot integrity" in defense of the statute, the judges said, was a lie. The restrictions were about race, not fairness or accuracy. It was old-fashioned Jim Crow work. Seemingly amazed, the judges noted that "neither this legislature, nor, as far as we can tell, any other legislature in the country has ever done so much, so fast, to restrict access to the franchise."[11]

I could go on. Federal courts also threw out the white caucuses' moves to effectively overturn Greensboro's city council elections in 2015.[12] Unhappy with the local voters' decision to produce a Democratic council majority, including four African American councilors, Republican legislators created new electoral districts, double-bunking (placing two existing officeholders in a single district) successful incumbents. Federal Judge Catherine Eagles saw through the ruse and invalidated the statute as yet another move to disenfranchise Black Tar Heels.[13]

During the same period, the General Assembly repealed the state's noted Racial Justice Act, which made it easier to attack death penalty sentences that were shown to be racially discriminatory.[14] Lawmakers also restricted civil race-discrimination cases in the state courts.[15] In response to the nationwide Black Lives Matter protest movement, they made it harder (not easier) to obtain access to police-camera videos.[16] Somewhat famously, white Republican legislators enacted a statute making it illegal for state agencies or local authorities to remove Confederate war memorials. A lead sponsor explained that the Civil War had nothing to do with slavery: "It was caused by the North and their tariffs over Southern goods."[17]

In 2020, the North Carolina House and Senate passed measures aimed at outlawing the "advocacy" of what they deem to be critical race theory in the public schools, though the measure was successfully vetoed by the governor.[18] Still, local school boards quickly got the message and began to limit what could be said and read in public schools.[19] Teachers began to express their fear and aguish under the censors' haunting specter.[20] And even more recently, Republican lawmakers outrageously threatened to impeach African American justice Anita Earls—undoubtedly one of the most highly credentialed and accomplished jurists ever to serve in North Carolina.[21]

Senate Republican leader Ralph Hise proudly explained that the General Assembly had, in a few short years, amassed "the most conservative record of any state legislature in the nation."[22] That's one way to put it. No doubt the white caucuses of the North Carolina statehouse have made dramatic progress in their apparent crusade to out-Mississippi Mississippi.

North Carolina, Race, Voldemort, and Constitutional Democracy

You would think that an all-white Republican governing majority in the statehouse regularly and demonstrably passing statutes to burden, handicap, harass, and punish Black citizens would become an intense and passionately contested focus of the political and social lives of North Carolinians. After all, it's not 1954. And this is North Carolina, not Alabama.

But that hasn't been the case. Though a racialized agenda has become foundational and normalized for our Republican legislative leaders, it's not something they talk about. Unlike tax cuts, deregulation, or slashing welfare programs, lawmakers on the stump don't boast about discriminating against Black people—at least not directly. Courts tell us that lawmakers lie about their racial intentions in the legislative deliberation process. And in the broader world as well, mum's the word. Many Tar Heels, maybe most, seem to think little or nothing of it—as if someone had quietly constructed an unstated, invisible bridge to the Jim Crow era. It's a strictly "hear no evil, see no evil" situation.

And this approach apparently requires a "speak no evil" component as well. In an odd twisting of the metaphor, the General Assembly's crusade against people of color is decidedly not to be mentioned—even by its critics. Somehow, it is thought to be too rude, too impolite, too confrontational to characterize a legislative program as race based no matter the facts or the findings. The theory seems to be that the mention of race implies that the folks carrying out the schemes to use state power to burden and handicap minorities are vile and reprehensible characters. Even if their work is race based, the label still shouldn't be applied. It's too barbaric, too unseemly. It is the "Voldemort" of modern North Carolina politics.

Even a bit player in North Carolina politics like me has had a good deal of experience with the phenomenon (as if the accusatory words of an elderly law professor are worth the political censor's energies).

Having written regular political columns for the *Raleigh News & Observer* and the *Charlotte Observer*—the state's two largest newspapers—for many years, I have, on occasion, had the bad manners to mention both the racial makeup and the oft-demonstrated racialized agenda of North Carolina Republican officials. Threats from legislators, a governor, UNC Board of Governors members, and university administrators have frequently followed. I would have thought it unseemly and modestly embarrassing for such powerful government officers to so energetically "shoot down" at a mere academic. Still, there resulted furious Republican caucus discussions, spirited legislative floor debates, gubernatorial declarations of outrage, offended lawmaker op-eds, harassing puppet think-tank "public records" requests, Board of Governors faux deliberations, academic center closings, and wounding law-school budget cuts.[23] Free speech, in the new North Carolina, is remarkably passé. If an agenda of racial subordination is so defining, so central, so base riling, so politically essential, then why keep it under wraps? The Grand Old Party "doth protest too much, methinks."

What drives this North Carolina crusade, so many years after the ratification of the Equal Protection Clause, to yet again use the power of government to intentionally burden and exclude African Americans and thereby purposefully further entrench the perennially preferred white majority?

The "who" pursuing the mission is sadly identifiable. First, it is clear that the racial animosity lodged in the heads and hearts of many North Carolinians is notably more pronounced and decidedly more pervasive than many longtime Tar Heels assumed—or, more correctly, more pervasive than longtime *white* Tar Heels assumed (Black folks, not so much). As I've indicated, the state has a well-crafted, if often inaccurate, reputation for moderation in the American South. There is, to be sure, something to this. North Carolina, for example, had Terry Sanford when Alabama had George Wallace. And Frank Porter Graham ran the University of North Carolina for decades. But the singular and horrifying racial massacre and coup in Wilmington, the forcible crushing of fusion politics to secure a hegemonic white supremacy after the Civil War, the stunning Tar Heel record of Black lynchings, the often nation-leading Ku Klux Klan membership, the Greensboro assassinations, the Wilmington Ten prosecutions, the aggressively enduring segregation of the state's public schools and universities, and much more give the lie to any actual claims of "moderation."[24]

The overt racism that has been apparent since Barack Obama's election, much fueled and energized by Donald Trump's ascendancy, finds solace—and extensive membership—in the Republican Party of North Carolina. Even if it doesn't reflect the majority of the state GOP rolls, it enjoys a solid and apparently secure home there. And it is apparently more potent, committed, and influential than the wider mainstream assumed.

But uncloseted racists aren't the bulk of the now-governing coalition. Most Republicans don't boast of a soul-crushing commitment to white supremacy; they are just eagerly (but mostly quietly) willing to firmly lock arms with those who do. They include what we used to refer to as country club Republicans—folks who vote solely on what they perceive to be their potential for expanded pocketbooks. As ever, they demand reduced taxes and increased subsidies for the wealthy and those who think, perhaps against all odds, that they soon will be. If that means they have to ride the backs of segregationists, then it's a small price to pay. Still, they insist, "I'm no Klansman—don't hit me with that. I just partner with Klansmen to fatten my wallet. My conscience is clear." And then there is maybe an even larger group: the ironically named Christian evangelicals. "We embrace racists in the cause of Jesus" is their unuttered claim. "Sometimes, you have to join with the hateful, the cruel, and the violent to serve the Lord; we know that Jesus seemingly favored the downtrodden, but we're convinced Christianity is really about homosexuality and abortion, and hard-core racists are our compatriots in such suppressive efforts—like us, they prefer to fly to New York for their abortions."

Equally expansive is the group of younger, modestly hipper libertarians—those who fervently believe that they're free from any obligations that are traceable to history or the broader society that surrounds them. Nothing is owed, nothing is triggered, nothing is demanded, nothing is relevant. They seem to be saying, "I am literally an island. What is essential is that I be left alone—especially now that my advanced degrees have been subsidized, my parents' money has been inherited, my craft's technologies have been developed at government expense, and my gated community has been secured. All we ask now is that government leave us be. We've got enough in store to deem ourselves the deserving fittest—though we may need the help of these odd, racialized folks to prevail in politics. We're not responsible for them though, or anything else, for that matter. Don't ask us any questions. Make upon us no demands."

I'm not sure, though, that there's any meaningful line to be drawn between the eagerly announced bigots and these three much larger and purportedly more respectable cohorts. All choose to betray the American promise out of animosity, greed, or insularity, which violate our actual creeds and constitutions. If someone were thwarting and abusing my kids, would it matter to me if they were the mover or the silent, allegedly blind partner? Those who demand white supremacy and those who put up with it, prosper from it, and rely on its intensity—for whatever reasons—kill the central meaning of our nation along with the interests and prospects of millions of our compatriots. And that problem, which has been long dominant in North Carolina's political life, has become the central challenge of the United States as well. So it's understandable, I suppose, that Republicans don't want their strategic partnerships and muffled crusades to be much discussed.

If, however, the membership rolls of North Carolina Republicanism are complex, variegated, and shifting, then the structures and practices of racial marginalization and subordination in the state are decidedly old school. As my good colleagues and North Carolina historians Jim Leloudis and Bob Korstad have recently written:

> In a pattern repeated multiple times, blacks and their allies have formed political movements to end racial discrimination and claim their rights as equal citizens. They have done so not only to advance their own interests but to promote participatory democracy more generally and make government responsive to the needs of all its people. Invariably, conservative lawmakers have countered such efforts by erecting barriers around the ballot box.[25]

In the decades immediately after the Civil War, Leloudis and Korstad note, North Carolina "conservatives called themselves Democrats, campaigned against government policies that redressed inequality and conspired to deny black men the right to vote, while Republicans identified as social progressives, championed a more expansive and generous state, and fought for universal male suffrage." Starting in the mid-twentieth century, the historians conclude, the "positions flipped."[26] Eric Foner, a scholar who specializes in the Reconstruction era, puts it this way: "The politics of today is continuous with the past that made it, marked by the struggles that have never really ended, only ebbed, shifted, and returned."[27]

Experts have characterized these now seemingly urgent electoral strategies as a race "against a rising tide of demographic change."[28] In North Carolina, the GOP holds a statewide advantage primarily because of its strong performance among older, non-college-educated, and non-urban white voters. But "the Republican edge is ebbing amid powerful demographic currents," most notably white-collar, urban newcomers and "the aging into the electorate of younger generations defined by a kaleidoscopic racial diversity."[29]

William Frey, an expert at the Brookings Institution, adds that Republican lawmakers like ours "see the wave of demography coming and they are trying to hold up a wall and keep it from smashing them . . . it's the last bastion of their dominance, and they're doing everything they can [to secure it]."[30] Most will see the United States become a minority-majority nation within their lifetimes.[31] For many white Americans, Leloudis and Korstad note, "these developments are the source of a profound sense of loss, a longing for the privileges once associated with skin color, a desire to make America great again, not surprising in a nation that from its founding defined white freedom in a way that necessitated black subjugation."[32]

Breaking the Compact

The Fourteenth Amendment to the United States Constitution, ratified in 1868, has proven to be the most consequential change ever made to our governing charter. It sets forth the following:

> All persons born or naturalized in the United States . . . are citizens of the United States and of the State wherein they reside. No State shall . . . abridge the privileges or immunities of citizens of the United States; nor shall any State deprive any person of life, liberty, or property without due process of law; nor deny to any person within its jurisdiction the equal protection of the laws.[33]

The North Carolina legislature considered the proposed amendment on two occasions. In December 1866, Tar Heel lawmakers rejected it.[34] Many claimed that it demanded "humiliating" and "dishonorable" terms.[35] One stalwart critic reportedly protested in private correspondence that federal proponents sought to "make us drink our own piss and eat our own dung."[36] A year and a half later, though, given relentless national pressures and altered state political realities, the provision was forwarded and ratified.[37]

Former representative John Bingham, the Fourteenth Amendment's principal author, explained that it set forth "a simple, strong, plain declaration that equal laws and exact justice shall be secured within every state for any person, no matter whence he comes, or how poor, how weak, how simple, how friendless."[38] It was meant to begin to remedy the tragic defects of 1789 and to bring egalitarian democracy to the United States.[39] Bingham also said, "We propose to put it into the power of every man, woman, child, black or white, rich or poor, when his rights are invaded, to raise his hand toward the flag, and say, 'I am an American citizen.'"[40]

Over the last decade, the Republican caucuses of the North Carolina General Assembly have sought, yet again, to reject this foundational premise of the American charter. Like their Civil War predecessors, they are so committed to their own ascendancy that they would set aside our defining democratic mission in order to retain it. Briefly put, regardless of their relentless homilies to a hollowed-out patriotism, they mean, tragically, to break our national compact. And the work hasn't stopped with intentional racial subordination.

In 2016, the Republican General Assembly enacted what the nation's leading election law scholar deemed "the most brazen and egregious political gerrymander yet seen in the United States."[41] Former representative David Lewis (who was later indicted on federal charges and pleaded guilty to dramatic campaign finance violations) explained: "I think electing Republicans is better than electing Democrats, so I drew the maps to foster what I think is better for the country."[42] He broke the rules to favor his friends, he said—and to disenfranchise his enemies—as much as humanly possible.[43] Ballot access, voter registration, and voting requirements were passed, which courts later ruled to be based on mere pretext because the state had "failed to identify even a single individual who had ever been charged with committing in person voter fraud in North Carolina." The judges said that lawmakers attempted "to conceal their true motivation," curing "problems that don't exist" to "entrench themselves."[44]

After Republican candidates lost the 2016 gubernatorial and attorney general races, lawmakers acted in a purportedly "emergency" special session to dramatically limit the powers of those now-disfavored offices. They eagerly cast aside the most foundational rule of a democracy—that if you lose an election, you accept the results and move on. Their actions foreshadowed the Trumpism to come in 2021. National commentators were shocked, saying that the North Carolina "legislative coup" was "the kind of thing one might expect to see in Venezuela, not in a U.S. state."[45]

Other equality norms were dispatched as well. Lawmakers determined that a person seeking an abortion had to undergo and pay for a mandatory sonogram, which the doctor was required to display to the patient while uttering a state-mandated script like a Stalinist apparatchik.[46] A bathroom bill meant to humiliate and threaten transgender Tar Heels spurred international boycotts and outrage.[47] Public officials were given stunning license to discriminate against LGBTQ+ citizens.[48] An ambitious cascade of laws attacking the independence of the North Carolina courts was enacted, and dissenting judges were threatened with impeachment.[49]

Traditionally respected boundaries of separation of powers were demolished. And, not infrequently, reviewing courts announced that lawmakers had lied about their purported justifications for transgressing constitutional standards.[50] In short, over the last decade, the Republican caucuses of the North Carolina General Assembly have waged a multifront war against democracy, equality, and truth itself. Of course, not all of these measures are related to race—though the lawmakers often seemed to begin with race before expanding their horizons. And once a crowd determines to favor its own predominance over its nation's defining purposes, subsequent barriers can be felled with relative ease. Race isn't everything in North Carolina, but it is, apparently, a window to everything.

From Breach to Sedition?

It can be stunning to contemplate what has happened over the last dozen or so years in North Carolina. American constitutional theorists almost uniformly assume that an array of guardrails, hard and soft, securely establish democratic government in the United States. Bruce Springsteen sings of the "flag flying over the courthouse," meaning certain things are "set in stone"—things like who we are, what we'll do, "and what we won't." North Carolina Republican lawmakers seem to have forgotten the "what we won't" do part. They're weak on the "who we are" and "what we'll do" commitments as well.[51]

To make the point, there are all kinds of folks in the United States— liberal and conservative; rich and poor; white, Black, Latinx, Native American, and Asian American; gay and straight; Republican and Democrat; religious and not; and millions more besides. These disparate members press their goals in the tough cauldron of electoral and representative politics. Sometimes, one group or set of groupings will prevail; sometimes, another will. Majorities change, as do attitudes and preferences.

But some things remain set in stone: the right to vote, majority rule, free and fair elections, freedom of speech and religion, equal protection under the laws, a necessary separation of powers, and an independent judiciary to keep the channels of democracy open and guarantee the rule of law. These are the essentials, the fundaments. They ensure that our defining commitment to democracy can actually be made operational. We may fight like hell over economic, environmental, and social issues, but these basics are meant to endure. These rules of the game define the democratic venture's meaning. They make sure it works—and lasts.

A lot of these barriers have been freely and purposely blown through in the last decade. Apparently, fewer people believed in them than many of us assumed. More seemed to think that they applied only to their adversaries and not to the "home team." And the barriers were softer, fuzzier than we'd hoped or needed. Traditions, patterns, and conventions—perhaps unwritten but nonetheless essential to the workings of democracy—have been surprisingly cast aside so that power-obsessed politicians could operate outside the lines. Constitutional democracy demands an array of mutual assurances. Too many North Carolina Republican leaders have tragically proven willing to break the common understandings in order to hold onto and augment their powers. Tar Heels knew, intellectually, that this could happen. It had happened here before. But, still, most of us didn't think it would happen again—not here, not now. We'd fight, in other words, about a lot of things, but not whether or not we would still strive to be a democracy. That broad and essential working assumption, it turns out, was wrong.

This book, however, is being written in 2022, after the massive, stunning, heavily racialized, violent January 6 insurrection at the nation's capitol—after the bulk of the Republican members of the United States House of Representatives voted, without a shred of authority or justification, to literally overturn the 2020 presidential election, and after a sitting president of the United States attempted to enroll the military, the national Departments of Justice and Homeland Security, Congress, the states, and millions of citizens in an unprecedented coup against the federal government. Can't it reasonably be said that in whatever ways North Carolina lawmakers may have broken our constitutive covenant, they are surely small potatoes in the age of Trump?

In some sense, that is surely true. Legislative leaders Phil Berger and Tim Moore haven't stormed the Capitol, attacked police officers, or plotted the brutal overthrow of the government. There is no equivalency here; it's true. But there is, crushingly, a decided kinship in the efforts. Both revolutionary campaigns rise from the same rejectionist soil.

Ponder it. Our Republican lawmakers have repeatedly, unconstitutionally, passed laws to disenfranchise Black Tar Heels. They have intentionally cheated, time after time, in the election process. They've overturned local elections because they didn't like the outcomes. They've refused to comply with the most basic rule of democracy—that is, if you lose, you turn over the keys to the new folks and try again next time. And each time they've done one of these things, they've lied about it. Don't take my word for it. Reviewing courts have explicitly said so over and over again.

What happens to lawmakers if they regularly attack American democracy and then dissemble about it? Do they explain to themselves that they've cast aside what they pledged allegiance to as children? And to accomplish that destruction, that they've had to cheat to get more power? And that it's been necessary to dissemble repeatedly because you can't exactly broadcast that you're out to overthrow our hard-won democratic traditions in favor of rule by a preferred, minority tribe? Given all that, is it really that big of a stretch to then try to invalidate a presidential election? How about insisting that state election officials literally steal thousands of votes? How about filing lawsuits to try to invalidate the votes of millions of Black citizens specifically? Is it really that different to storm the Capitol or try to kill your way into power? I think not. Or, more relevantly, I'm convinced that they think not. As in the South of the nineteenth century, we have a massive group among us that is willing to throw democracy aside in order to ensure its ascendancy.

And once again, this diseased North Carolina politics increasingly stains the broader land. Perhaps Tar Heels didn't originate the democracy-destroying illness, or uniquely define and export it, but we live it. We embrace its handiwork. Millions of us apparently long for it. We work to entrench and deepen it—to make it thrive. We adhere to it, with a patent defensiveness, but without remorse. And the pattern aggressively asserts itself across Dixie and beyond. Like Jefferson Davis and Robert E. Lee, we're willing to trade its demeaning allure for America itself.

Rosanell Eaton

When I was younger, I would have been more certain about the cures for such existential challenges. Potential statutes, constitutional amendments, judicial interventions, electoral alterations, legal standards, and partisan campaigns would spring quickly to mind. But I'm older now. After a lifetime of study and engagement, I find it hard to place meaningful confidence in the courts, state or federal. I now worry more about judicial efforts to thwart democracy rather than to protect it. And legislative prospects to secure "the blessings of liberty," here or in Washington seem distant and pale—or worse. My optimism and hope have altered over the decades. And its locus has evolved.

Rosanell Eaton died in 2018 at the age of ninety-seven in her hometown of Louisburg, North Carolina. The *New York Times* eulogized her as a "fierce voting rights advocate," having fought to make the promises of democracy real in her home state for more than seven decades.[52] I was honored, if somewhat intimidated, to share a platform with "Mother Eaton" a couple of times at Moral Monday and NAACP protests. I remember her straightforward explanation for a lifelong struggle against Tar Heel voter suppression: "It's obvious. It's planned. They want to think, here, that the world belongs to a certain race of people and they don't want the rest of us to be equal."[53]

She wouldn't put up with it.

Rosanell Eaton experienced the terrors and degradations of Jim Crow in North Carolina. One of seven farm-family children, she was a veteran of segregated schools, bathrooms, and water fountains.[54] As the valedictorian of her high school class, her defiance began early. At age twenty-one, she sought to register to vote in Franklin County. Three white officials taunted her, explaining that she'd have to recite—from memory—the preamble to the United States Constitution. She didn't blink and proceeded to set out the paragraph perfectly. "Well little lady," one responded, "you did it."[55] She then became, in 1942, one of North Carolina's first Black voters since Reconstruction.

Eaton joined the NAACP in 1950, participating in and helping lead protests against racial discrimination for many decades. She registered thousands of voters, served as a county poll worker, and did a stint as a special registrar. As a result, Eaton and her family were regularly threatened with violence. Night riders burned crosses outside her home. Bullets were fired into her farmhouse, striking her bedroom window. Again, she wouldn't yield. As her daughter Armenta explained, "She [wasn't] afraid of anything."[56]

Rev. Dr. William J. Barber II, who has long been North Carolina's and is now the nation's leading civil rights and antipoverty leader, asked Rosanell and Armenta Eaton to be lead plaintiffs in a federal case challenging North Carolina's racially restrictive voting laws in 2016. Rosanell had been protesting against the measure for more than three years. Now in her nineties, she testified boldly. She reminded both the people of North Carolina and the courts that "we have been this way before."[57]

This was hardly the first time that white North Carolina lawmakers had lied in order to disenfranchise Black Tar Heels. "She would often tell us that the reason she had to fight now was because she had to fight then," Reverend Barber explained.[58] The judges struck down the statute, ruling, "We cannot ignore the record evidence that, because of race, the legislature enacted one of the largest restrictions of the franchise in modern North Carolina history."[59]

Then-president Barack Obama paid tribute to Mother Eaton in a 2015 interview:

I was inspired to read about unsung heroes like Rosanell Eaton in Jim Rutenberg's "A Dream Undone." . . . I am where I am today only because women and men like Rosanell Eaton refused to accept anything less than a full measure of equality. She has not given up. She's still marching. She's still fighting to make real the promise of America.[60]

More than once, Reverend Barber told a story about walking with Eaton to a demonstration outside the General Assembly building in 2013. She moved slowly, aided by a walker. Barber told her, "Rosanell, you don't have to do this." She replied, "I know what I have to do."[61] That she did.

The late Howard Zinn explained long ago that what matters are the countless small deeds of often unknown people who lay the basis for the significant events of human history. "They are the ones who have done things in the past, they're the ones who will have to do them in the future."[62] Maybe it wasn't accurate, by the end of her life, to think of Rosanell Eaton as an "unsung" hero. She had been lauded in national publications and feted in the White House. But she certainly didn't start out that way, or long for it, or carry it in her expectations back when she was riding a mule cart in rural eastern North Carolina, registering people to vote. And when I would watch her from the throngs at protests, it was clear that, as she led, she gave testament to her commitment. There was no doubt about that. But even more powerfully, I thought, she taught. She instructed, not just by her words, but by how she stood, how she paused, and how she pronounced her phrases, unbowed. I thought she was saying always, "Let me show you something. Let me teach for just a minute." This is what it means to be, and to fight for, and to live in "first-class citizenship," as Fannie Lou Hamer used to put it. And it doesn't matter what others choose to think, or how they might dismiss you, or what nastiness they might hurl. "This is what you do. Watch. Learn a little something—something big, something real, something that matters."

I wouldn't bet against the Rosanell Eatons of North Carolina. Neither should anyone else.

CHAPTER TWO

★ ★ ★

Politics, Tribe, and
(Unchristian) Religion

n early January 2012, Rev. Dr. William J. Barber and the North Carolina NAACP, the North Carolina Justice Center, and the poverty center I ran at UNC–Chapel Hill (until it was closed by Republican leaders) launched what we called the "Truth and Hope Tour of Poverty in
North Carolina." The bus tour was comprised of four two-day journeys
across North Carolina over an eight-month span, taking a hundred or so
preachers, journalists, authors, professors, social workers, organizers, activists, students, government officials, and do-gooders to every corner of
the state. After visiting about thirty communities and meeting with many
thousands of low-income and often desperate Tar Heels, the tour concluded with a spirited August summit in Rocky Mount, a town in eastern
North Carolina. The experience was one of the most powerful of my life.

During the bulk of the tour, North Carolina was in the throes of a much
different sort of campaign as well—the electoral struggle to accept or reject Amendment 1, a proposed state constitutional ban on same-sex marriage. Gay marriage was already illegal in North Carolina at the time, having long been banned by statute. Still, proponents heatedly proclaimed
the restrictive measure's necessity, and the Tar Heel State eventually became the last in the nation to ratify such a provision, not long before all of
the state equality-denying marriage prohibitions were declared unconstitutional by the United States Supreme Court.[1]

A significant percentage of the folks on the poverty tour lived in the
Triangle region of central North Carolina (Raleigh, Durham, and Chapel
Hill). During the Amendment 1 campaign, the Triangle was abuzz with

a weighty, seemingly pervasive, and almost uniform opposition to the anti-gay-rights measure. Signs decrying the proposed constitutional alter-ation were everywhere—every street corner, highway, public park, restau-rant, retail business, and public accommodation and many residential front yards in between. Rallies and demonstrations demanding the refer-endum's defeat were constant and relentless. And although statewide polls still seemed worrisome, it became possible to think, based on everything folks in the Triangle could see, that perhaps, against the odds and all pre-dictions, the prohibition of same-sex marriage might be defeated at the polls.

The early legs of the poverty tour headed from Raleigh into eastern North Carolina—the poorest region of the state. The first town meet-ing was held in "little" Washington, in Beaufort County. We then moved to Roper in Washington County and to Elizabeth City State University in Pasquotank County, which is in North Carolina's northeastern coastal corner. Caravans then backtracked into rural Hertford and Halifax Coun-ties and convened large gatherings in more urban Edgecombe County. To be sure, eastern North Carolina communities didn't reveal the same glut of apparent opposition to Amendment 1 that Durham and Chapel Hill residents had become used to and could be deceptively buoyed by. But still, signs of antagonism toward the proposed constitutional change were pronounced and enthusiastic, even if not uniform or commanding, like they seemed back home. A subsequent southeastern tour segment, visiting Lumberton, Red Springs, Fayetteville, Wilmington, Pender County, and (coastal) Brunswick County, seemed broadly the same. The tour itself, of course, was exposing, exploring, documenting, and agitating against poverty in the Tar Heel State. But those, like me, who were also active in the crucial work of attempting to defeat the amendment, could remain heartened.

But the optics changed notably when the tour headed west weeks later. One of the tour's final legs, somewhat inaccurately labeled the "West-ern North Carolina Tour," left Durham with stops in Mount Airy, Went-worth, Salisbury, Hickory, East Spencer, and Hendersonville. We also held urban meetings in Greensboro and Charlotte. Almost as soon as

the buses passed through Orange County (Chapel Hill) and headed into
rural Alamance County, the Amendment 1 landscape became dramatically transformed. Billboards, small and large, hand painted or commer-
cially produced, carefully spread apart or lumped together into massive
accumulations, appeared everywhere in support of the anti-gay-marriage
measure. More surprising, at least to me, was the relentless array of rural, Protestant churches that boasted not one, or two, or a half-dozen
pro–Amendment 1 signs—including, often, very sizeable ones—but
sometimes an attention-grabbing forty or fifty or one hundred messages,
designed to announce, I guessed, that there was no confusion or dissent in
each congregation. God was mentioned regularly in the missives. I quickly
reminded myself that one comes to know little of North Carolina by hanging out in Durham or Chapel Hill. Once again, I feared for equality's prospects in my home state, and I fretted for the plight of my LGBTQ+ fellow
citizens.

As a result, though, I was moderately less surprised when, a few weeks
later, Billy Graham himself, who had generally enjoyed at least something of a reputation for staying on the sidelines in political disputes while
working with all presidents and parties, took out a full-page ad in fourteen
newspapers across the state, saying:

> At 93, I never thought we would have to debate the definition of
> marriage. The Bible is clear—God's definition of marriage is be-
> tween a man and a woman. I want to urge my fellow North Caro-
> linians to vote for the marriage amendment on Tuesday, May 8. God
> bless you as you vote.[2]

Graham's decidedly less-beloved son, Franklin, in the meantime, blan-
keted the state with radio ads, urging all to "take a stand on God's definition of marriage."[3]

The eventual electoral results were brutal. Sixty-one percent of Tar
Heels voted for Amendment 1.[4] We thus became the thirtieth state to en-
shrine a prohibition of same-sex marriage into our local constitution. Our
provision was notably ambitious, declaring "marriage between one man
and one woman is the only domestic legal union that shall be valid or rec-

ognized in the state." Tami Fitzgerald, chairwoman of Voter FOR Marriage NC, the amendment's principal sponsor, explained: "You don't rewrite the nature of God's design for marriage based on the demands of a group of adults."[5] In a peek at what was to come, election officials noted that this was "the craziest election" the state had seen in decades, with proponents of the amendment "challenging and confronting precinct officers," demanding to act as poll watchers, sometimes aggressively contesting the right of various people to vote, and "pushing to get officials to get people to show their IDs in order to vote" even though that wasn't required by law. We've apparently got a lot of folks in North Carolina who claim to speak for God. And sometimes they get mad on his behalf as well.

Of course, the United States Supreme Court invalidated same-sex marriage bans in the 2015 case *Obergefell v. Hodges.*[6] But that didn't seem to end the matter for North Carolina lawmakers. In April 2017, the Uphold Historical Marriage Act was introduced by still-committed same-sex-marriage opponents. The proposed bill, authored by four Republican members of the House, declared that the *Obergefell* ruling was "null and void in North Carolina" because only a marriage between a man and a woman "shall be valid or recognized" in the state, citing Amendment 1. The act also attempted to defy *Obergefell* by announcing that all "marriages between persons of the same gender" are invalid—even those performed outside the state.[7] Its authors explained that "the United States Supreme Court overstepped its constitutional bounds" in the landmark decision. North Carolina, in their view, shouldn't put up with it.

Ultimately, the Uphold Historical Marriage Act didn't pass in the House. A similar proposal put forth by another group of Republican representatives in 2019, which sought to outlaw the United States Supreme Court's supposed "parody marriages," suffered the same fate.[8] Senate Majority Leader Phil Berger, however, had already had better luck.

Legislating Religion

In 2015, following the *Obergefell* ruling, Phil Berger pushed through a groundbreaking law that allowed any North Carolina magistrate to refuse to marry and any register of deeds to refuse to issue marriage licenses to any couple that the public official has "a seriously held religious objection to serving."[9] These state judicial officers, therefore, literally need not afford "equal protection of the laws" to all Tar Heels. We now have, as a result, two tiers of judicial actors: those who are required to follow the Fourteenth Amendment and those who can opt out by claiming special rights to escape constitutional obligation. Religious folks are afforded unique privileges that are enjoyed by no others. They don't have to obey certain legal claims that they object to. Law is permissive for them but binding for everybody else. Their creed immunizes them; it provides them with safe haven. The special-exemption law's terms are open ended, ostensibly offering protection to "religious" beliefs that demand racial and other forms of invidious discrimination as well. In practical terms, though, Berger's law is meant to elevate exclusionary "Christian" dogma over the general applicability of the rule of law. "Serious religious" jurists can cast aside and humiliate members of the polity whom they disapprove of—just like they did in the good old days. They are free to declare to marital partners whose relationships they don't approve of, "Sure, you may pay my salary, and this may be the United States, but you'll receive no equality, no dignity, no decency here—only derision and disdain in this government office—because my personally declared religion trumps your citizenship."

Republican representative Larry Pittman, one of the bill's primary sponsors, explained that "state employees should not be required to sanction something they consider perverted and morally unconscionable." He added:

> There is no way anyone can support anything other than what God made marriage to be. We at least ought not to be forcing people to be participating when they believe that to do so would make them traitors against the kingdom of God.[10]

"Traitors against the kingdom of God." Good Lord. So much for a magistrate's oath of office. We now have regular judges who enforce the law and right-wing Christian jurists who are free to choose whether they want to follow the law or not. Their personal preferences are more important than the mandates of American constitutional government so long as their "religious" predispositions conveniently mirror conservative politicians' own.[11]

Subsequent measures became even more extreme. In 2016, the Republican-dominated General Assembly, in an absurdly designated special session, passed the internationally infamous House Bill 2 (HB2), or North Carolina's "bathroom bill."[12] In a move to pander to right-wing social and religious conservatives and to demonstrate disdain for transgender Tar Heels, lawmakers went where no American government had gone before or since. HB2 demanded that people use public building restrooms that correspond with the gender reflected on their birth certificates, thus barring many transgender residents (and visitors) from restrooms that match their identity. No state had ever taken such a stance.[13] The statute also abolished a Charlotte ordinance outlawing discrimination based on sexual orientation and gender identity.[14] Critics deemed it, immediately, "the most anti-LGBTQ legislation ever enacted."[15] Gigantic protests and hugely damaging boycotts erupted across North Carolina, the United States, and the globe.[16] The federal government sued North Carolina to protect the constitutional rights of its transgender citizens. Intense wounds to the equality and dignitary interests of marginalized citizens were sustained and billions of dollars were lost.[17] The traditionally nurtured image of North Carolina as a moderate southern guidepost was permanently demolished. Under astonishing and enduring external pressure, the brutal measure was partially repealed in 2017.[18]

Persons identifying as evangelical Christians provided the strongest base of support for HB2. Some 68 percent said transgender folks should be forced to use the bathroom of the gender that is reflected on their birth certificates.[19] Tami Fitzgerald, executive director of the NC Values Coalition; Rev. Mark Creech, head of the Christian Action League; and other Christian conservative organizations ran an impressive phalanx of support for the anti-trans statute. The bill's principal sponsor, Dan Bishop (then a state representative and later a U.S. congressman), sneered at what he called "a cross-dresser's liberty." The "safety of women" was being "subverted and sacrificed" by men pretending to be women, in his view. Bishop labeled opponents of HB2 a "Taliban" of "extremists," declaring that "the

LGBT movement jeopardizes American freedom."[20] For Bishop, "a small group of far out (radicals) shouldn't presume to decide matters for the rest of us." He said he was unperturbed by international opposition "because I don't fear man, I fear God."[21]

Bishop had partnered readily with the Alliance Defending Liberty (ADF), a right-wing evangelical organization that has been identified by the Southern Poverty Law Center as an anti-LGBTQ+ hate group, to crusade for HB2.[22] The ADF claims that it "was founded to defend religious liberty and fend off the ACLU's efforts to immobilize Christians."[23] Republican former governor Pat McCrory, defending the controversial bathroom measure, echoed Bishop's disdain for the supposed rights of "boys who might think they're a girl."[24] Republican leader and State Sen. Buck Newton brought the discussions full circle in celebrating the passage of the landmark anti-LGBTQ+ statute, announcing, "This is the day the Lord has made, we won't bow and kiss the ring of their political correctness theology."[25] Newton also claimed HB2 was necessary "to keep our state straight."[26] The line of separation between white evangelical Christianity and government in the state of North Carolina is, I fear, a thin and permeable one. And the mark that the marriage of politics and a particular brand of Christianity leaves on our social and political well-being appears to be neither a generous, affirming, constructive, nor congenial one.[27]

The Oddest Agenda

A February 2020 Elon University poll concluded that 30 percent of North Carolina voters reported themselves to be white evangelical Christians.[28] In the November 2020 election, 80 percent of white evangelicals in the nation and 82 percent of white evangelicals in North Carolina voted for Donald Trump.[29] National polls suggest that white evangelical Christians are far less likely than other Americans to believe there is systemic racism in the country.[30] They are also apt to be more critical of the Black Lives Matter movement and less condemning of racist rhetoric than other Americans.[31] Robert P. Jones, president and founder of the Public Religion Research Institute, has characterized white evangelicals as "nostalgia voters," hearkening back to a 1950s America "before *Brown v. Board of Education*, desegregation and the civil rights movement," when white Anglo-Saxon Protestants were more dominant demographically, politically, and socially. The "backward pull is the real attraction," Jones asserts.[32] Most Americans think that police actions toward Black people are often discriminatory, but "white evangelicals overwhelmingly do not." They are also reported to be the only major religious group to believe that Islam is at odds with American values.[33] And perhaps most astonishingly, white evangelical Christians are far more likely to support gun rights than other Americans.[34]

The Elon study also found that white evangelical Tar Heels tend to be more opposed to raising the minimum wage, more opposed to government programs that provide affordable housing, more opposed to the Patient Protection and Affordable Care Act, and more likely to have a favorable view of the fairness of the American economy than other voters. A breathtaking 89 percent favor a photo identification requirement in order to be able to vote. Nicholas Kristof has written that "young and middle-aged Americans could be forgiven for thinking that Jesus was a social conservative who denounced gay people and harangued the poor to lift themselves up by their bootstraps, until he was crucified for demanding corporate tax cuts." Rev. William Barber has called this "theological malpractice": "Some folks hijacked Christianity and decided that they were going to put up a lot of money to promote the idea that to be a person of faith was to be anti-choice, anti-gay, pro-gun, pro tax cut."[35]

The Sermon

I'm not one to talk much about religion. Nor would I be inclined to criticize one's Christianity. I grew up Catholic but decided decades ago that the Catholic Church makes it too difficult to hold on to your membership and your conscience at the same time—not a good trait in a religion. Besides, after I reached my twenties and began studying matters in earnest, I realized I couldn't make myself believe in most of the essentials. So, unlike Reverend Barber, I'm not competent or fit to theologize.

But, that being said, I've long been taken with the Sermon on the Mount. I'm not saying that I'm stout enough to live by it; I'm decidedly not. But I grew up understanding it to be the greatest distillation of the teaching of Jesus known to us. And, even in my cranky old age, I find it to be the most astonishing grouping of words ever assembled. Let me remind some of its core:

And he opened his mouth and taught them, saying:

Blessed are the poor in spirit, for theirs is the kingdom of heaven.
Blessed are they that mourn, for they shall be comforted.
Blessed are the meek, for they shall inherit the earth.
Blessed are they that hunger and thirst for righteousness, for they
    shall be filled.

Blessed are the merciful, for they shall obtain mercy.
Blessed are the pure in heart, for they shall see God.
Blessed are the peacemakers, for they shall be called children of God.

After declaring his kinship with the marginalized, wounded, and dispossessed, Jesus then turned to the stunning spirit of his message of love, generosity, and conciliation.

You have heard it said, "Thou shall not kill."
But I say unto you that whosoever is angry with his brother without
    cause shall be in danger of judgment.

You have heard it said, "An eye for an eye, and a tooth for a tooth."
But I say to you resist not evil; whosoever shall smite you on the
    right cheek, turn to him the other also.

And if any man will sue you at law and take away your coat, let him
    have your cloak also.
Give to him that asks of you, and him that would borrow from you,
    turn not away.

You have heard it said, "Thou shall love thy neighbor and hate
your enemy."

> But I say love your enemies, bless them that curse you, do good
> to them that hate you, and pray for them that despitefully use
> you.... Judge not that you be not judged. Your Father in heaven
> makes the sun rise on the just and the unjust.

Finally, Jesus closed with perhaps the world's most eloquent call to material renunciation.

> Lay not up treasures on earth, where moth and rust corrupt, and
> where thieves break through and steal.
> For where your treasure is, there will your heart be also.

> Behold the birds of the air: for they neither sow, nor reap, nor stow
> in barns, yet your heavenly father feeds them.

> Consider the lilies of the field; they neither toil nor spin,
> yet even Solomon in all his glory was not arrayed like one of these.

> Take therefore no thought for the morrow, for the morrow will take
> thought for itself.
> And it came to pass, when Jesus had ended these sayings, people
> were astonished at his doctrine.[36]

Tribe over Both Creed and Constitutionalism

I'm not out for a religious battle. Perhaps it is enough to say that the chasm between the political agenda of most white Christian evangelicals and the teachings of Jesus is wide—beyond wide. It might even be fair to say, ironically, that the gulf is more dramatically pronounced than is the case for any other mainstream political grouping in North Carolina (or the United States). It can almost bring to mind Frederick Douglass's statement, though obviously made in a radically different context: "Between the Christianity of this land, and the Christianity of Christ, I recognize the widest possible difference."[37] White Christian political evangelism seems to borrow only the naming figure of the New Testament gospels and not the doctrine. The Sermon on the Mount ends by announcing that "the people were astonished at his doctrines." The evangelical Christian political movement, on the other hand, seems to reject those doctrines outright. "We'll march in Jesus's name," the theory seems to go, "but we care not a whit for what he said and stood for. In fact, we organize principally to oppose those tenets. We are, in short, political evangelicals who work and remonstrate robustly against policies aligned with the teachings of Jesus. Don't let the name confuse you. And don't forget that there are a lot of us. And we mean to have things our way."

I haven't found it easy to get my head around these contradictions. I fear, of course, that they are the heirs of older, even more horrifying traditions. Southern Christian ministers and politicians famously used the Bible to sanction slavery. Jim Crow, too, often enjoyed the church's embrace.[38] Perhaps more directly and more specifically, years ago, when I began (in my own amateurish way) to study the 1961 Freedom Rides, I was much taken aback by the link between the brutal terrorism waged against the demonstrators and churches—or, at least, church members. In his book about the Freedom Rides, Raymond Arsenault, when recounting the attacks in Anniston, Alabama—where beatings and burnings almost killed the nonviolent riders—notes that the Sunday morning assault was led not only by local Klansmen, but by white Christian church members in Anniston, "having just come from [church services] dressed in their Sunday best—coats and ties and polished shoes." A few "even had their children with them" to join in the murderous ambush.[39]

Alan Cross's research came to similar conclusions about the Montgomery bus attacks. "Men, carrying baseball bats and lead pipes, were holding the Freedom Riders back and women were hitting them with their purses and holding up their children to claw at their faces." Cross, a Protestant minister who grew up in Mississippi, sought to learn "why the white Christians didn't show up" to stop the horrors. He determined, to his life-changing dismay, that "many of the people in the white mobs were themselves regular church members." The lesson for Reverend Cross was so powerful that he has made it a crucial, though sometimes unpopular, component of his ministry.[40]

I'm not trying to equate the atrocities of the Freedom Ride assaults with the particulars of white, Christian evangelical politics in 2022. They're not parallels. But, for years, I've contemplated the reality of folks leaving the Sunday services of their Christian churches—dedicated, in theory, to the teachings of Jesus—to attempt to maim and murder Black and white nonviolent bus riders. The commitment to tribe, to the white Christian hegemony of the South, readily, conclusively, violently, and unapologetically, outweighed the very doctrine of the Sermon on the Mount. The Freedom Riders, no doubt, challenged a way of life, a people, a tradition, a "tribe" of long-empowered whites. The rioters, in extreme and obviously demonstrable form, assaulted and wounded others on behalf of their particular group. Clubs and baseball bats were thought necessary to secure what was "expected" and "deserved," what was "owed" or "owned" in their lives. They used shocking violence to protect a long-asserted ascendancy, to secure "us" from "others."[41]

Fifteen years ago, I was president of the College of William & Mary. During my brief tenure, I made what became an immensely controversial decision to alter the way a Christian cross was displayed in the college's Wren Chapel. William & Mary is a public university, and its chapel, which is the cornerstone of the campus, is used regularly for important secular college events—both voluntary and mandatory. I determined that the large cross should no longer be permanently placed on the altar but, rather, displayed only during requested religious services. I did so believing the step to be necessary to help Jews, Muslims, Hindus, nonbelievers, and other religious minorities feel more meaningfully included as members of the broader college community. I was convinced, as well, that a reasonable notion of separation of church and state required the decision.[42] No small number disagreed.[43]

There were many strands of opposition. One of the largest and most surprising to me, as a state university official, was essentially a claim of tribalism. For example, my critics complained, in one phrasing or another:

> If I had gone to the Cardozo School of Law, I would not have bridled or balked at seeing Jewish symbols; or if I had attended Notre

Dame, I wouldn't mind Catholic icons; if I were to go to college in Saudi Arabia, I would not expect people to remove symbols of Islam; I would not attempt to empty out the Vatican. Why then do they not give the same deference to OUR schools? When I go to the Jewish community center, I don't expect them to change. If Muslims, Jews, Buddhists, or atheists are offended by this, then, frankly, that's too bad.[44]

"People of faith," another person wrote, have "given up too much, yielded too many of our founding sacrifices and histories.... I am offended that outsiders would accept an invitation into our culture and then demand that we change it." It's okay, another wrote, "if they come, but they should not ask that we alter our way of doing things."[45] We "cannot cringe in fear to those who object to our Christian traditions, giving in to the spiritually egalitarian crowd in the worship of multiculturalism."[46]

I've come to think that these sorts of comments reflect much of the heart of North Carolina's white evangelical Christian political movement: We've given up too much that is ours. We're the ones who really count. These strangers might be allowed to come here or stay here, but we're the core; we're the owners. Others may enter and be tolerated, but we're the special ones; we are the people whom the United States and North Carolina were made for. We have always been in control, and we must remain so. It doesn't matter what the Constitution says. It doesn't even matter what Jesus said. We're the chosen ones. If we are asked to choose between the American experiment and our own ascendancy, it's not a close call. We're all in for our tribe—and only our tribe.

CHAPTER THREE

Politics and Poverty

I n February 2022, the North Carolina General Assembly debated the size, scope, and future of the free and reduced-price lunch programs in public schools. Republican state representative Mark Brody lit into school nutrition officials. "I think the job of this General Assembly is to force you to go back to basics and put your personal agenda aside," he said.[1] Brody made clear his existential opposition to "government-sponsored meals." He indicated, "I go to my food banks and there's lots of food going on." Nobody is being "denied anything, the idea that kids don't have access to good food—parents just need to buy it and feed it to them . . . my mother did that to me."[2]

Republican state senator Ted Alexander harmonized: "Don't parents really have the responsibility, at any income level, for ensuring that their children have food, or are we, as a government, sending the message that they're incapable of doing that so we'll do it for them?" Republican state representative Jamie Boles Jr. took the inquiry to what he apparently thought was a moral high ground: "I just think we're leading toward a socialization that takes the responsibility away from the families," he fretted.[3] I'm not completely sure what Representative Boles meant by that, but I don't think he was speaking in support.

The declaration of such sentiments is not a rare or isolated occurrence among North Carolina Republican lawmakers. U.S. senator Richard Burr famously slandered low-income parents seeking health care for their children as "hogs at the trough."[4] His colleague Thom Tillis turned the hostility into a strategy, "a way to divide and conquer the people who are on assistance."[5] Tillis proclaimed, "We need to get folks like that woman with cerebral palsy to look down on [other] people on assistance, saying we may end up taking care of those babies, but we're not taking care of you."[6] Former U.S. representative Robert Pittenger overtly racialized the sentiment, saying that Black protesters in Charlotte were "enraged because they hate white people who are successful," adding that government had spent too much money on welfare programs "that ultimately hold people back."[7]

Former state representative Craig Horn declared that a program he had helped to enact that required drug tests for Work First recipients was necessary because "a large segment of the population that receives welfare benefits either abuses the system or does not use the benefits for the purpose intended."[8] (The statute's mandated pilot program emphatically disproved Horn's claim. Yet the testing measure was retained.)[9] Former state representative Michael Speciale, a Republican member of the General Assembly from New Bern, explained his enthusiasm for increased work requirements for food assistance recipients, saying, "short of telling them 'you can sleep all week,' how much more reasonable can you get?"[10] In 2015, Sen. Norman Samuelson explained that it was necessary, despite soaring hunger and unemployment rates, to limit food stamps for families in the state's most hard-pressed counties—even though food stamps are completely paid for by the federal government—because recipients needed a shove to go to work. "I think you're going to see a lot of them go out and get that twenty-hour-a-week job now," he predicted.[11] And most famously, State Rep. George Cleveland, from Onslow County, asserted in a formal House committee meeting that "there is no extreme poverty in North Carolina"; the federal government merely pads "agency figures to justify a poverty level that they want." There's "no real deprivation here."[12]

Representative Cleveland somehow missed that nearly 10 percent of the children in his Onslow County district live in extreme poverty (on incomes of less than $13,000 per year for a family of four).[13]

These unmoored ideological assumptions, which often undergird harsh public-policy decisions in North Carolina, bump jarringly against the actual facts of poverty and economic hardship in the Tar Heel State.

North Carolina countenances extraordinary levels of poverty. For perspective, the United States, tragically, lets more of its citizens live in wrenching poverty than almost any other advanced, democratic nation.[14] We are also the most unequal major nation in the world. Thomas Piketty, who has taught so much about yawning and dangerous economic inequality, wrote a few years ago that inequality in the United States right now is "probably higher than in any other society, at any time in the past, anywhere in the world."[15] Let that sink in.

Americans are also particularly tough on our kids. Though we're the richest country in the world, we have the thirty-second-highest child poverty rate of the thirty-eight Organization for Economic Co-operation and Development (OECD) countries. We lag far behind Denmark, Norway, Sweden, and Iceland, of course, but also behind the major European nations—Germany, France, Ireland, Austria, Portugal, Switzerland, the Netherlands—and British Commonwealth countries like Australia, Canada, New Zealand, and the United Kingdom, not to mention South Korea, Lithuania, Greece, and Mexico.[16] As the U.S. special rapporteur on poverty and human rights determined, the United States is the "clear and constant outlier on child poverty."[17] Some bragging rights those are.

And North Carolina is, on average, even worse. About one in five Tar Heel kids (19.5 percent) live below the federal poverty threshold (about $25,000 per year for a family of four). That's the tenth highest rate in the nation. Almost one in ten of our kids lives in extreme poverty. The youngest segment of our state's population is the poorest. Twenty-two percent of children five years old and younger are impoverished. Child poverty is also highly racialized. Children of color are three times as likely as white kids to be poor. And child poverty in North Carolina, in recent decades, has become decidedly more heavily concentrated, with poor kids living in neighborhoods that contain higher and higher percentages of other poor folks. Children are thus increasingly required to deal with not only their own family's economic hardship, but also those of their community. Their economic mobility, as a result, has notably suffered, making it more likely that if they are born poor, then they will stay that way. Tragically, our youngest and most vulnerable face the most daunting economic challenges.[18]

The picture of North Carolina's child hunger is similarly bleak. The state's food insecurity rate is one of the country's worst. In most North Carolina counties, at least one in five kids are food insecure; in twenty counties, the rate is more than one in four. Hunger is racially skewed, too. While 62 percent of white households with kids are food secure, only 43 percent of Black and Latinx households are. More than 250,000 households with children participate in the federal Supplemental Nutrition Assistance Program (SNAP)—food stamps. Nearly six in ten Tar Heel public-school students are enrolled in the free and reduced-price lunch program. Despite Republican lawmakers' potently uninformed rhetoric, hundreds of thousands of North Carolina children, year in and year out, don't get enough to eat.[19]

So, first, it should be said that political leaders like Representative Brody get it wrong about food banks. As my colleague Dr. Maureen Berner, who actually studies the North Carolina food bank system, reports, "The need for food assistance is vastly unmet; the system lacks the capacity to meet current and future demands."[20] Peter Werbicki, who runs the massive and much decorated Food Bank of Central and Eastern North Carolina, has noted that if they took the food they distribute each year in all thirty-four counties they cover and redirected it "entirely to only Wake County, it still wouldn't meet the need, even there."[21] Alan Briggs, former director of the NC Association of Food Banks, put it this way:

> The gap between what food banks can provide and the depth of the hunger we face is gigantic, it is way too big, it can't possibly be bridged. I ask parents to think, when they sit in line to drop their kids off at school, that one in four of those innocent kids going into the schoolhouse isn't getting enough to eat. And then to remember all the problems that hunger triggers: harm to health, harm to cognitive ability, harm to learning, harm to ability to concentrate.[22]

The remarkable Rev. Jim Summey, pastor and executive director of High Point Community Against Violence, echoes Briggs's conclusions:

> Private charity can help conditions for some and those efforts deserve support and recognition. But the magnitude of the problem

is unimaginable and unquantifiable. A line we often hear from food banks and pantries is some version of this: you can double, triple, quadruple our budget, and we could reach more people and distribute more nutritious food, and we'd do it well and efficiently. But we'd still only be scratching the surface.[23]

To be clear, I'm fairly certain that if Representative Brody was made fully aware of the facts of childhood hunger and food access in North Carolina, it wouldn't change his rhetorical claims one whit. He's chosen his horse, and he'll keep riding it.

My point, though, is a broader one. My friend Clyde Fitzgerald, longtime executive director of the Second Harvest Food Bank of Northwest North Carolina, died three years ago. He explained to me, more than once, that in "North Carolina hunger doesn't manifest itself like it does in Africa, with people falling to the ground and dying before our eyes." For many of his friends, Fitzgerald said, "that's the vision they have of hunger, and they prefer to keep it that way." They're convinced that there's no actual hunger here because they don't see it. "I always tell them, if you've got a half-hour, come on with me, I'll show it to you...but they invariably decline."[24] I've heard similar reports from poverty workers across North Carolina—in inner-city Charlotte, in the woods of Hickory, in homeless camps under the bridges of Fayetteville, in trailer parks in Wilkesboro, in soup kitchens in Greensboro, in shelters in Boone, in food pantries in Bertie County, in community action agencies in Jacksonville and Goldsboro, in low-income clinics in New Bern, and in men's overnight facilities in Elizabeth City. The list is long. Folks deny the existence of hardship, and then they don't want to be shown otherwise. It's something of a pattern. Most of us seem to embrace it—especially our lawmakers.

A lot of low-income folks in North Carolina understand the disconnect, though they don't necessarily assume good faith. Cynthia L., whom I came to know at Crisis Assistance Ministry in Charlotte, complained:

You know these people who say they don't know about the poverty in this city, how can that be?...It's impossible not to see it. On my way downtown to work, I see it every day. There's somebody sleeping

on every bench. How do you not know about it? You don't want to
know. People living in a park, people waking up outside. They want
to keep saying Charlotte's a great place to live, just be careful not to
cross the train tracks. Don't tell me you don't know, it's pure denial.
I won't live that way.[25]

Others hope that leaders might be willing to change course if they knew
more about the difficulties that folks actually face. Stacy Sanders, who has
served as the Fayetteville Police Department's liaison to the local homeless community, is "tired of hearing people say we don't have these kind of
problems; we have to take the blinders off and quit pretending it doesn't
happen here."[26] Dr. Evan Ashkin, who treats low-income patients at the
Prospect Hill Community Health Center in Caswell County, reports that
the arguments he hears from lawmakers, that poor Tar Heels are often
freeloaders who want to game the system and get free medical care, reflect
a "viewpoint that is possible only if you've never worked with anyone in
this patient population." His patients are waiters, gardeners, farmhands,
motel workers, dishwashers, day laborers, and home health care workers.
Maybe policymakers ought to come down the road a few miles, he says,
"and get to know them."[27]

But whether the ignorance is purposeful or negligent, the outcome is
the same. Having some of the developed world's highest poverty rates,
child poverty rates, and child hunger rates is, for us, not problematic and
not worrisome. It triggers no meaningful, majority-sponsored, state antipoverty initiatives. Instead, crushing benefit cuts for low-income Tar
Heels ensue, shredding our already meager social safety net protections.
Just as disheartening, we behave as if having deplorable child poverty levels is as natural as a Carolina tide. Who cares if we treat our kids worse
than almost anyone else? Why should that draw our attention? We apparently have bigger challenges on our minds—daunting worries like the
bold threat of critical race theory being taught in grammar schools, the
haunting prospect of transgender folks showing up in bathrooms or on
little league teams, or the risk of pesky scientists publishing data about
the ocean's rise. We can't be bothered with the likes of poor and hungry

babies. But as Thomas Paine wrote in *Common Sense*, "a long habit of not thinking a thing wrong gives it the superficial appearance of being right"—even when it's wrong, deadly wrong.

Punishing Poor People

When Republicans secured unfettered control of all three branches of North Carolina government in 2013, they quickly passed a cornerstone of their economic policy agenda—literally gutting the state's unemployment compensation program, ensuring that it became the most tightfisted plan in the country. It still is. The principal architect of the unemployment "reform" was State Rep. Julia Howard. She announced that the state's traditional unemployment approach was much too generous and had effectively "become a welfare scheme."[28] Labor experts had a different opinion, calling the enacted changes "a radical reduction in benefits for people unemployed through no fault of their own." Within five years, only 8.6 percent of Tar Heel jobless workers were receiving unemployment. That ranked the state fifty-first in the nation (when the District of Columbia and Puerto Rico are included). And North Carolina's average duration of benefits for those few who do qualify had dropped to the country's lowest. In 2018, Wayne Vroman, an expert at the Urban Institute, explained in a legislative committee hearing that our worst-in-the-nation program tragically underserves the state's workers. Republican lawmakers, though, were thrilled with the "last-place" designation. Former state representative Dana Bumgardner, a Gaston County Republican, replied without irony, "I think where we are is a good thing. What is the point of your presentation?" There are no regrets about trailing the whole pack; quite the contrary, there is cause for celebration.[29]

The unemployment compensation demolition was soon swaddled by an array of massive cuts to programs and policies meant to (modestly) support low-income Tar Heels. The *New York Times* decried the "decline of North Carolina," denouncing the wrenching damage wrought by the Republican majority on "the economically distressed and marginalized."[30] Most painfully, lawmakers refused to accept the Medicaid expansion of-

fered under the Affordable Care Act. Congress thought that the Medicaid
"offer" it had made with Obamacare was one no sensible state government
could refuse. That assumption was true but not dispositive. Refusing expansion, which has gone on for more than a decade, has cost North Carolina tens of billions of federal health care dollars, hundreds of millions
in state and local revenue, hundreds of thousands of jobs, and billions of
dollars in lost federal payments for uncompensated care. Even more ruth-
lessly, studies indicate that thousands of poor Tar Heels have died as a result of the horrifying Medicaid decision.[31]

North Carolina also soon became the only American state ever to
abolish its earned income tax credit, thereby raising the tax bill owed by
roughly a million Tar Heel families that make about $35,000 per year.[32]
The Center on Budget and Policy Priorities determined that the North
Carolina General Assembly had merited the "dubious distinction" of being the only American government ever to move in this fashion to make
it harder for low-income families to support their kids.[33] Next, lawmakers initiated a series of tax policy changes designed to shift the burden
away from the wealthy and lodge it more significantly on the poor.[34] They
scrapped the progressive income tax, adopting a flat rate. They did away
with the estate tax, which only applied to estates of $5 million or more.
They cut tax rates for out-of-state corporations and wealthy individuals
while expanding sales taxes that hit poor folks disproportionally.[35] And
they cut pre-kindergarten education, child care, dental care, food stamp,
and legal aid programs on which the most distressed rely. North Carolina
Republicans earned a national reputation for their willingness to step on
the necks of poor people.[36] And they seemed to enjoy it.[37]

The depressing policy changes came in an array of fields—labor, education, health care, child support, access to justice, and tax assessment. They
shared, though, the same undergirding, inaccurate, ideologically based
assumption: that poor Tar Heels are unworthy. They assert that anyone
who is unemployed, unable to secure health insurance, or otherwise unable to make ends meet is lazy, irresponsible, uncommitted to their family,
bereft of ambition, devoid of character, anxious to game the system, and
enthusiastic to live off the generosity or naivety of others or, even worse,

the government. The legislative declarations that opened this chapter drip with the disparaging sentiment. Republican lawmakers in North Carolina know virtually nothing about the lives and challenges of poor Tar Heels, but they are willing to fill that unfortunate informational void with a heavy, persistent, animosity-driven, factually irrebuttable set of predispositions about the worth of their low-income peers. They seemingly cling to the regime of marginalizing assumptions regardless of how the world actually unfolds. Circumstances may change; antipathy to poor people abides.

To take a rather stunning example of the phenomenon, consider the horrors of the Covid-19 epidemic—a torrent of death, unemployment, and disease arising some seven years after the legislative enactments of 2013. The North Carolina General Assembly didn't cause the pandemic, of course, but its policy determinations made it immensely more difficult for Tar Heels to successfully respond to the disease. A national study from late 2020 found that an astonishing 5.4 million Americans had, by then, lost their health care coverage as a result of pandemic-caused unemployment—likely the steepest increase ever recorded.[38] The researchers concluded that nearly half (46 percent) of all increases in the ranks of the uninsured resulting from the Covid-19 pandemic occurred in five states: California, Texas, Florida, New York, and North Carolina. By then, eight states counted more than one in five of their adults as uninsured, including Texas, Florida, Georgia, Mississippi, Oklahoma, and, again, North Carolina.[39] Tar Heels, who lost their jobs by the hundreds of thousands, had to cope with the stunning and dangerous change of fortune via the worst unemployment compensation program in America. And the massively overloaded North Carolina health care system was burdened even more powerfully by the exclusion of more than a half-million poor Tar Heels per year as a result of the unexplained and inexplicable refusal to accept billions of federal health care dollars under Medicaid expansion.[40]

But, tellingly, even when the General Assembly met during the worst throes of the pandemic, with large budget surpluses at its disposal, lawmakers refused to budge on unemployment compensation and Medicaid. During those sessions, Tar Heel lawmakers knew, without a doubt, that thousands and thousands of their fellow citizens had lost their jobs and access to health care, frighteningly, unavoidably, and through no conceivable fault of their own. No one could have sanely believed that North Carolina workers had suddenly, en masse, become lazy and shiftless freeloaders, temperamentally unwilling to work or support their families. Still, Republican lawmakers clung stubbornly to their ideological markers. "Don't bother us with the facts or the tragedies of our constituents," the theory seemed to go, "our political religion demands commitment to the principle that poor people are worthless and morally deficient." "We've drawn our terminally wounding line in the sand," the General Assembly seemed to say. No further discussions were to be required or tolerated. "Ignore the plights of your families, your neighbors, your communities," they effectively claimed. "Our ideology is what matters"[41]—even when it is clearly wrong, perhaps especially when it's clearly wrong. Through a marriage of unemployment woes and health care miseries, millions of North Carolinians were left to face a brutal plague with neither compensation nor care even though the lawmakers knew, undeniably, that their foundational bases for rejecting national norms in health care and worker protection were demonstrably untrue.[42]

The Denial of Full Membership

Of course, the Covid-19 pandemic taught North Carolinians much more than the naked pretense of lawmakers' decision-making. The disease had not only wreaked havoc on life here and across the country in ways that could scarcely be imagined; it has also fallen heaviest on the poor and Black and brown people. "Essential" but somehow expendable workers were forced, by the hundreds of thousands, to risk exposure to the virus while their more advantaged and more highly resourced neighbors enjoyed relative safety through isolation. Nearly two-thirds of the highest-paid quartile of wage earners were allowed to work remotely during the pandemic while only one in ten of the lowest-paid quartile of the workforce enjoyed that luxury. Across North Carolina, beleaguered low-income workers were disproportionally forced to report in person to risky workplaces while being paid salaries that didn't actually cover the basic costs of supporting their families. And hundreds of thousands more lost their jobs, their incomes, and their ability to feed and house their children, without the slightest fault or warning.[43] The virus strained and stressed multitudes who did not have adequate reserves on which to rely. And it threatened the bodies of those whom the state callously excluded from one of the most unequal health care systems on the planet. In other words, there could not have been a more patent, tragic, concrete, and irrefutable illustration of the yawning chasm of inequality that characterizes life in North Carolina.[44] Once again, the bottom third, economically, were treated as if they didn't count—or at least didn't count as much as the rest of us. Thurgood Marshall famously argued in *Brown v. Board of Education* that the "infant appellants" he represented sought to assert "the most important claims that can be set forth by children . . . the right to be treated as entire citizens of the society into which they have been born."[45] Poor Tar Heels had been shown, once again, that they are not "entire citizens" of this storied commonwealth.

Lesser citizens, those who are not "entire," need not be consulted in governing decisions—nor do their concerns or voices have to be taken into account. It is unimportant whether they thrive or diminish. They are not actual members of the constituency. They are the disappeared, or the never existent. Their "betters" can feel free to proclaim what is best for them—even if their declarations have no actual correlation with the challenges that they face. They are the unworthy; so are their children. We have no responsibility toward them—no kinship and no obligation. Their lack of virtue disqualifies them even if their asserted lack of virtue is a demonstrable and demonstrated lie. They should be seen as strangers to our constitutions and creeds because our obligations set forth there do not apply to them. It is more important that we be freed from guilt over the breach of our platitudes than that they be afforded a meaningful chance. It has, seemingly, ever been so, and thus it must remain. If we are the richest, the poorest, and the most unequal society on earth, it must be because we have the most worthless and therefore dismissible constituents. They are not of us.

But as Reverend Barber has put it, in two of the best sentences I've read in some decades, "We cannot allow people in power to be comfortable with other people's deaths. We just can't allow that anymore."[46]

CHAPTER FOUR

Destroying a Priceless Gem[1]

The most famous words ever uttered about the University of North Carolina came from Tar Heel–born journalist Charles Kuralt. Delivered at a 1993 bicentennial celebration in Kenan Memorial Stadium, before a huge audience that included then-president Bill Clinton and former governor Jim Hunt, Kuralt opened by saying, "I speak for all of us who could not afford to go to Duke, and would not have even if we could have afforded it."[2] Not long after came the much-replayed refrain:

> What is it that binds us to this place as no other? It is not the well or the bell or the stone walls. Or the crisp October nights or the memory of dogwoods blooming. Our loyalty is not only to William Richardson Davie, though we are proud of what he did two hundred years ago today. Nor even to Dean Smith, though we are proud of what he did last March. No, our love for this place is based on the fact that it is, as it was meant to be, the university of the people.[3]

Powerful words. Marvelous ones. But, of course, Kuralt's short, optimistic narrative starkly ignores the University of North Carolina's largest sin against democracy, against equality, against any purported mission as a "university of the people"—its brutal record, as a southern state institution, of discrimination, especially race and sex discrimination, against an extraordinarily high percentage of its people.[4]

UNC was the nation's first public university, founded at New Hope Chapel Hill in 1793.[5] But it was an all-male institution until 1897, when a handful of female applicants were admitted. Enrollment had increased to only four hundred women by 1940, almost none of whom were freshmen or sophomores. By 1962, women constituted 22 percent of the student body. Women moved from the periphery only in 1972, with the passage of the federal Higher Education Act's Title IX, when the total number of enrolled women climbed to 6,500.[6]

The federal courts ordered the admission of African Americans to the UNC School of Law in *McKissick v. Carmichael* in 1951.[7] The first three Black undergraduates were admitted in 1955, after *Brown v. Board of Education* was handed down.[8] Despite these legal commands, the enrollment of Black students remained exceedingly low for many years. In 1960, four Black freshmen enrolled at UNC–Chapel Hill. As late as 1963, there were only eighteen.[9] Three decades later, Edwin Caldwell Jr. (the great-grandson of Wilson Swain Caldwell, a heroic North Carolina educator who was held as a slave by UNC's president at the time, David Swain, until the conclusion of the Civil War),[10] said, "I don't understand this … why does everything got to go to court to get people to do what's right? And the university has been one of the last [to admit Black students]. You have always got to run to court before doing what's right."[11]

As the reference to Wilson Swain Caldwell reminds, the crushing student and faculty exclusion is but a part of a far more chilling and unyielding story. My former student Geeta Kapur movingly and powerfully documented the fabric of racism that has worked to define the university at every moment of its 230-year history.[12] In a recent federal civil rights suit, a federal court encapsulated UNC's racial history in the following finding:

> Southern historian Dr. David Cecelski provided credible evidence that UNC "has been a strong and active promoter of white supremacy and racist exclusion for most of its history." Over the centuries, the university's leaders have included the state's largest slaveholders, the leaders of the Ku Klux Klan, the central figures of the white supremacy campaigns of 1898 and 1900, and many of the state's most ardent defenders of Jim Crow in the twentieth century.[13]

Like many institutions, in other words, the University of North Carolina's embrace of equal protection was almost nonexistent for the bulk of its history, and that breach dramatically wounded the prospects of the state, the school, and Carolina's most vulnerable people. Nor, accordingly, could it accurately raise the banner of a people's institution.

Still, the tragedies of unacceptable, if widely shared, historic exclusions do not, in my view, disable or eliminate the University of North Carolina as a potential source for understanding what a public university ought to be. In a way, that conclusion mirrors the broader study of American constitutional development. Our constitutional framers set in place a remarkable set of mechanisms to ensure liberty, equality, dignity, self-governance, and deliberative democracy. The great flaw in the undertaking was that the government's inclusive umbrella extended only to white (and perhaps only propertied and Protestant) men. The most generous view of American history is as an unfolding—the too slow, too grudging, too costly, too tragic, but continuous expansion of the full protections of constitutional participation to a broader and broader membership of the polity. Accordingly, the standards and operations of constitutional democracy carry a fuller credence in decidedly more congenial modern times. The same is true, I would think, for the mission and purpose of the American public university. Its goals tug ever more profoundly as state universities reject and eventually move to overcome their initial and mission-defeating exclusions.

And on this front, Carolina has much to teach about the meaning and purpose of public universities. UNC carries the mark of William Richardson Davie, Edward Kidder Graham, Howard Odum, Frank Porter Graham, William Friday, William Aycock, and a cadre of other remarkable leaders. In 1936, the *New Republic* wrote that "North Carolina [had] become the leading institution of higher learning in the south." Writing about the 1940s and '50s in his masterwork *Speak Now against the Day*, John Egerton concluded that "the single most glaring exception to the broad-based mediocrity of the southern academic world was the University of North Carolina." For more than two centuries, North Carolinians have spent energy, talent, and character to build a flagship university as a public good. Progress has hardly proven linear, but it's been more than significant.[14]

The University of Alabama's higher education scholar Wayne Urban wrote, only a few years ago: "The University of North Carolina is a storied institution with a storied history. It serves as a kind of beacon for scholars in the rest of the South, a place that sets a standard to which other institutions in the region, especially their faculties, can aspire."[15]

A beacon can be crucial, Urban noted, "since the life of the mind is in an unhealthy state throughout the South." When a wide chasm exists, he explained, between the seeming consensus beliefs of a state's political leadership and the "core intellectual values of its faculty members," the intellectual climate for public universities becomes "stark."[16]

On Public Obligation and Academic Integrity

North Carolina's first state constitution declared "that a school or schools be established by the legislature for the convenient instruction of youth, with such salaries to the masters, paid by the public, as may enable them to instruct at low prices, and all useful learning shall be duly encouraged in one or more universities."[17] The constitutional provision was followed in December 1789 by a statute chartering the University of North Carolina: "In a well-regulated government, it is the indispensable duty of every legislature to consult the happiness of a rising generation and endeavor to fit them for the honorable discharge of their social duties of life, by paying the strictest attention to their education."[18] A "university supported by permanent funds and well endowed, would have the most direct tendency to answer the above purpose."[19] Fittingly, the university was chartered only a few days after North Carolina ratified the United States Constitution.[20]

William Richardson Davie had pushed the General Assembly for the statute and became the University of North Carolina's principal founder. Davie believed that "only through the establishment of first class academies and a state university" could the "self-government and liberty attained through the revolution" be preserved.[21] A post–Civil War constitutional provision codified a defining commitment to economic access: "The General Assembly shall provide that the benefits of the University of North Carolina, as far as practicable, be extended to the people free of expense" (article IX, section 9). Frank Porter Graham, UNC's most consequential president (1930–1949), offered a charge in his inaugural address "to build in this region one of the great intellectual and spiritual centers of the world for even the poorest youth."

An economic democracy in the student body, though, has not been seen as the only component of an engaged public university. As then-president John F. Kennedy explained to UNC students at Kenan Memorial Stadium in 1962, this remarkable "institution has required great sacrifice by the people of North Carolina, I cannot believe that all of this is undertaken merely to give an economic advantage in the life struggle."[22] Former UNC president Edward Kidder Graham (1914–1918) thought it essential that a public university embrace the Progressive Era notion of the mind in service to society. He described UNC's campus boundaries as extending to the borders of the state and implored Tar Heels to "send us your problems." Graham urged his academic colleagues to escape the "cloister" and "release the educational principles and scholarly ideals of the university into channels of service" so that it would become an "instrument of democracy for realizing the high and healthful aspirations of the state." Journalist Jonathan Daniels wrote, in the mid-twentieth century, "The university grew in stature by getting down closer to the earth and examining the human qualities of the state and the south."

That required a particular focus, in Frank Graham's words, "on the plight of the unorganized and inarticulate, unvoiced millions." Howard Odum, perhaps the university's most defining scholar, controversially explored appalling conditions of poverty, farm tenancy, cotton culture, and rural illiteracy "to expose the facts, encourage reform, smooth social change, [and] make democracy effective in the unequal places." Former UNC president William Friday (1956–1986) would be even more direct in his focus, calling it crucial "to turn the university's mighty engines loose on the lacerating issue of poverty in North Carolina."[23]

UNC's leaders have also attested that if a vibrant democracy cannot exist without powerful and effective public universities, then vibrant state universities cannot exist without an equal commitment to the values and processes of democratic liberty. So long as public universities are funded and controlled by legislatures, they'll be uniquely subject to political tampering. A robust and renewed commitment to academic independence is thus essential. Frank Graham, again, claimed, "Without freedom there can be neither culture, nor democracy; without freedom there can be no university." Academic liberty, he wrote, "means the freedom of the scholar to report the truth honestly without interference by the university, the state, or any interest whatsoever."[24]

The 1963 Act to Regulate Visiting Speakers (or the Speaker Ban Law), which prevented purported communists from speaking on campus, represented UNC's greatest ever challenge to academic freedom. Former UNC chancellor William B. Aycock, in response, defiantly stumped the state, demanding repeal. He said, bluntly, "It would be far better to close the doors of the university than to let a cancer eat away at the spirit of inquiry and learning." He issued an urgent national call as well:

> Generation after generation have gone forth from this campus to provide sound leadership throughout the length and breadth of the land. It is a pity so many have left us for other places. We need them now. The University of North Carolina has come a long way fathered by rebellion and mothered by freedom. We may be short on cash, but we're long on freedom.[25]

If it is true, as I've suggested, that the essential markers of a great public university—or at least of one great public university, the University of North Carolina—have included defining commitments to student access regardless of wealth, the adoption of the felt needs and challenges of the commonwealth as part of its academic agenda, the examination and critique of social and public policies that have been demanded for informed democratic decision-making, and a robust commitment to the ideals of academic freedom and independence, then there is little doubt that, over the past decade, an array of these core components have been thrown into direct jeopardy in Chapel Hill. In some instances, worrisome signs demonstrate that earlier, consensus-based commitments are presently in fast retreat. In others, reversals seem even more purposeful and more demonstrably wounding to the mission, character, and quality of the university. They therefore pose a growing threat to what is likely the state of North Carolina's greatest intellectual resource and the nation's most instructive lodestar on what a public university should be. As a formal study committee of the American Association of University Professors (AAUP) found in the summer of 2022:

> The University of North Carolina is in trouble, and not the kind of trouble that record enrollment or good rankings can fix. It is the kind of trouble that festers and metastasizes.... [This report] details patterns of political interference by the state legislature into the administration of UNC, overreach by the Board of Governors and Boards of Trustees into specific campus operations, outright defiance of principles of academic governance by campus and system leadership, institutional racism, and a chilly climate for academic freedom. The cumulative effect of events, especially since 2010, leaves UNC in a precarious position.[26]

The cascade of political assaults directed against the University of North Carolina over the last decade also mirrors and amplifies ideological and partisan attacks on flagship state universities that have been seen increasingly across the United States, profoundly jeopardizing one of the nation's most prized assets: a broad-based, accessible, and accomplished system of public higher education.

Closing a Poverty Center

Before Republicans took control of the General Assembly in 2010, North Carolina lawmakers had generally sought to make moderate appointments to the UNC Board of Governors, maintaining a degree of partisan balance on the university governing boards that they oversaw. But with the 2010 ascendancy, that decidedly changed. Appointed members became more uniformly Republican, they were more apt to be active ideological partisans, they were more often former officeholders or lobbyists, and they had less previously demonstrated interest in higher education. In 2016, the sea change became official as outgoing governor Pat McCrory signed legislation stripping his Democratic successor of the power to make appointments to campus-level boards of trustees. The new statute shifted campus gubernatorial appointment powers to the legislature itself, and the American Association of University Professors reported that "the UNC system board of governors stands alone as the only statewide governing board that is solely appointed by the legislature without input from the governor."[27] Similar steps have been taken to capture the power to appoint members of community college boards.[28]

The new, more highly politicized UNC Board of Governors officially announced its agenda of partisan interference with the operation of the statewide university system in January 2015 by firing its highly respected president, Tom Ross. In a stunning, almost farcical press conference, former board chairman John Fennebresque could offer no reason whatsoever for the decision. "The Board believes President Ross has served with distinction, his performance has been exemplary, he has devoted his energy, intellect and passion to fulfilling the duties and responsibilities of his office . . . the decision has nothing to do with President Ross' performance or ability to continue in office." But, somehow, it was necessary to fire him. Apparently, it turned out, Ross was a Democrat. Fennebresque seemed as incompetent and disingenuous as he was partisan.[29] But the point was no doubt strongly demonstrated—a new group of sheriffs had arrived. The board launched its subsequent campaign against academic freedom on the Chapel Hill campus several months later with the closing of a poverty center that I directed. Tampering with the operations of the Center on Poverty, Work, and Opportunity, though, had begun a good deal earlier.[30]

I'm a constitutional lawyer by trade. In that capacity, I've published books and academic journal articles on judicial review, civil rights, constitutional theory, and the power of the federal courts for many years. But for the last two decades, I have concentrated heavily on America's wrenching challenges of poverty and economic justice. And over the same period, I've elected to publish not only in traditional law reviews, but also in the public press. While I taught at the University of Colorado, I became a columnist for the *Rocky Mountain News*, and for the more than two decades that I've been in Chapel Hill, I have written regularly for the Raleigh *News & Observer*, the *Charlotte Observer*, and other major North Carolina papers. I have intentionally sought to address issues of constitutional magnitude, typically involving questions of inequality, in the public arena of the state that I love and in which I reside. I doubt I'll shake the habit.

That has meant that, with some frequency, I have written articles and essays that challenge or criticize policies and practices that have been launched in Raleigh and Washington, D.C. (or earlier, in Denver, Colorado). This has, on occasion, irked and annoyed both university and government officials. But with the Republican capture of the North Carolina General Assembly a dozen years ago, accompanied by the launch of perhaps the stoutest and most substantive war on poor people carried out by any state legislature in a half century, tensions markedly increased.[31]

Throughout 2013, I wrote an extensive, year-long series of articles for the *Raleigh News & Observer* documenting the challenges of poverty in North Carolina. And both before and after the series appeared, I wrote a long cascade of articles and essays criticizing the policies and practices of North Carolina's governor and General Assembly, especially as they related to poor people and persons of color. Officials in both Raleigh and Chapel Hill were not amused.[32]

So, on at least a half-dozen occasions between 2012 and 2015, Jack Boger, the dean of the UNC School of Law, who was strongly supportive of my right to freely publish, felt compelled to call me into his office to inform me of threats he had received from Republican leaders of the General Assembly or then-governor McCrory's office concerning my publications. The proffered coercion was straightforward and direct: If I didn't stop publishing articles in the *Raleigh News & Observer* and the *Charlotte Observer*, I would either be removed as the director of the university's privately funded poverty center, the center would be closed outright, or I would be fired. Lawmakers demanded, Boger explained, that I formally agree to stop writing articles for the two largest newspapers in the state. The "ban" would apply to no other faculty member or administrator in the university system—only me. I refused to comply, repeatedly.[33]

Additionally, in August 2013, I was scheduled to speak at a large Moral

Monday protest in the Queen City. As I drove into Charlotte, I received
a call from the dean's office explaining that legislative leaders had informed him that morning that if I were to speak, significant negative consequences would follow. Boger, though, made no request that I refrain. I
spoke as I had at dozens of other Moral Monday and NC NAACP protests.[34] I'm old and tenured and, by now, somewhat thick skinned. The
sun still rose the next morning.

Months later, I published an article (in the forbidden papers) criticizing the governor's decision to sign what voting rights scholars called the
most restrictive electoral access law passed in a half century. Extensive
public records requests from right-wing advocacy groups followed, seeking thousands of my emails, phone call records, text messages, appointment calendars, and correspondence (regardless of the subject matter or
personal nature of the emails). Newspapers reported that the governor
had complained about my writings to campus administrators and Board
of Governors members. UNC's then-provost James Dean Jr. called and
emailed me, explaining that then-chancellor Carol Folt "had been under
a lot of pressure" at the statehouse because of my published articles. Dean
requested that I include a disclaimer on my publications indicating that I
do not speak for UNC. A few days later, I was informed by university officials, in writing, that my publications had "caused great ire among the governor's staff and close supporters." Though, the letter indicated, "there is
no present intention within the university to end your tenure as director
of the poverty center, the Chancellor, Provost and Board of Trustees must
necessarily be alert to the prospect of real injury to the university." It continued, "[we] hope that external forces will not combine in coming days
to circumscribe UNC's institutional autonomy or its tradition of faculty
freedom, but some of the forces in play lie beyond our control."[35]

Pointing out the absurdity of the requested disclaimer, I asked the uni-
versity how it was supposed to work; how broadly was it to be applied?
Not long before, I had published articles in the *Harvard Journal of Law
& Public Policy* and the *Duke Journal of Constitutional Law & Public Pol-
icy*. Another piece was soon scheduled for release in the *Wake Forest Law
Review*. I asked, "Am I supposed to put a disclaimer on those?" Of course

not, it was explained to me. No one cares in the slightest what I write in some Harvard journal; nobody in North Carolina reads that. Apparently, it was only when I published in the *News & Observer* or the *Charlotte Observer* that it was necessary to reveal that my employer detests me.[36]

To no one's surprise, the disclaimer provided only temporary solace. The actual annoyance was that I kept writing articles in the local papers. In August 2014, former governor McCrory signed a budget bill directing the UNC Board of Governors to review all "centers" within the expansive university system (there were 237) in order to find $15 million in savings. Newspapers across the state reported that, whatever else might occur in the review process, there was no doubt that the poverty center would be shuttered, even though closing an entirely privately funded center would generate no savings whatsoever. After going through a massive and fraudulent review charade, the Board of Governors voted in February 2015 to close the Poverty Center and North Carolina Central University's Institute for Civic Engagement and Social Change, which was also a privately funded venture and a frequent partner of the Poverty Center. Neither former chancellor Carol Folt nor former provost James Dean objected to the closure—the days of courageous leadership in Chapel Hill were long gone. Former state senator Bob Rucho, who played a major role in appointing the Board of Governors and, oddly, sat in the audience as board members voted to ditch the center, keeping a close eye on his charges, told local newspapers that it was necessary to shut the center "because Nichol was advocating anti-poverty measures . . . that we're opposed to." As if to emphasize the point, some months later the Republican General Assembly cut the law school's budget by $500,000 in what lawmakers called the "Gene Nichol transfer amendment."[37]

Republican lawmakers had warned, quite explicitly, for nearly three years that unless I stopped publishing articles in the *News & Observer* and the *Charlotte Observer*, the Center on Poverty, Work, and Opportunity would be closed. I didn't stop writing. They then made good on their persistent promise.[38] They punished me and the Poverty Center's students and employees because I refused to stop publishing clearly constitutionally protected expression. I've been teaching constitutional law for more than forty years, and I'd say, with a good deal of confidence, that no First Amendment lawyer in the United States thinks that particular set of government interactions is even arguably permissible. "Stop writing core, protected, First Amendment speech, or we'll use state power to punish you" was the explicit threat. They then carried out, methodically, precisely, and exactly what they said they'd do. It's legal to regulate universities and professors in many ways, but not in that way.[39]

Expanding the Assault

And the UNC Board of Governors was just getting started.

When I was dean of the UNC School of Law, I spent more than a year trying to coax Julius Chambers to come to Chapel Hill and establish a civil rights center. Chambers, the famed civil rights lawyer, was retiring as the chancellor of N.C. Central University. He was also, by a good measure, the UNC law school's most accomplished graduate. Chancellor Chambers, to my great delight, eventually agreed to come, but I remember that he warned me: "If we do our work well, the university will close us down. They're not going to let first-rate lawyers represent poor Black people." It turned out he was right.[40]

The center was launched at the law school in 2001. Chambers developed a community lawyering model at the center, teaching students and staff attorneys to help disempowered communities in North Carolina. It successfully litigated an array of racial discrimination, school desegregation, local government, and environmental justice cases across the state. Students loved the experience that it afforded, and lawyers admired Chambers's innovations. Unsurprisingly, the Republican-led Board of Governors was less enthusiastic.

In 2015, Steven Long, a Board of Governors member who had previously served on the board of the Civitas Institute (a right-wing think tank funded by Art Pope), began a multiyear effort to ban the Center for Civil Rights from litigating. Long was unimpressed, apparently, by the American Bar Association's demand that law schools provide significant clinical experiences to ensure expanded opportunities for "experiential learning."

Long may have known precious little about the demands of legal education, but he was certain that he didn't like the kinds of cases that the civil
rights center pursued.[41] As Ted Shaw, the center's director after Chambers
retired, put it, "The one thing that is clear to me about Long is that he is
someone who has an antipathy to the work we do on behalf of black and
brown people."[42]

When the Board of Governors convened in July 2017 to take up the
proposed litigation ban, the president of the Southern Association of
Colleges and Schools Commission on Colleges, UNC's accreditation
agency, appeared at the meeting to warn against undue influence by state
legislators and other politicians.[43] The AAUP president, Rudy Fichten-
baum, published an op-ed arguing that the board should oppose "a brazen attempt by one member of the Board of Governors [Long] to prevent the center from [representing] North Carolina's most vulnerable
citizens ... in a deeply troubling departure from longstanding principles
of academic freedom."[44] Nevertheless, the Board of Governors voted to
adopt the ban, ending the central educational mission of the Center for
Civil Rights and overruling the positions of the law school faculty and
dean, the UNC–Chapel Hill faculty assembly, the provost, and the chancellor. The center's two staff attorneys were immediately dispatched. Steve
Leonard, the former UNC System faculty chair said, "We've now reached
a point where the Board of Governors is acting in ways that interfere with
faculty prerogative on curriculum, research and service.... If we don't
stand up now and at least try to maintain the authority we have over these
matters, we're going to be in rough shape going forward."[45] The political
operatives of the Board of Governors were unmoved. Their Republican
patrons in the General Assembly were, once again, well pleased.

In 2021, the Board of Governors removed Eric Muller, one of the university's most accomplished scholars and teachers, from the governing board
of the University of North Carolina Press.[46] Muller had served two five-
year terms on the board, with the last six as chair. He was so well regarded
by his colleagues that he had been unanimously endorsed for reappoint-
ment by the press's board of directors and Chancellor Kevin Guskiewicz.
Without explanation, the Board of Governor's University Governance

Committee removed Muller from the recommended appointment slate. It was reportedly the first time that a recommendation by a campus nominating committee and the chancellor had been cast aside. No one at the press had been contacted by the Board of Governors. When the press's board asked for an explanation of the decision, the Board of Governors refused. UNC System president Peter Hans said, disingenuously, that he couldn't "speculate" about the board's motives or rationale. Others did. One (unnamed) member of the Board of Governors explained to *NC Policy Watch*:

> Muller has had a target on his back for a couple of years. There was a lot of anger that a prominent law professor [would criticize] the deal [made by the Board of Governors] with the Sons of Confederate Veterans over [the] Silent Sam [statue]. Professors are supposed to be teaching classes and not making statements to the press about what we do.[47]

Nor was any notice or justification given to Professor Muller himself. He inquired about the reasons why he had been singled out by the board:

> I would hate to think it had something to do with my [published] commentary on matters of law, race and history, such as the law on removal of Confederate monuments, the abortive $2.5 million settlement with the Sons of Confederate Veterans, the moratorium on renaming UNC buildings, or the removal of the portrait of slave-trading judge Thomas Ruffin from the courtroom of our state's highest court. I would hate to think it had to do with focusing attention on ways in which law has ignored and harmed the interests of African Americans. As a legal scholar and historian, this is [the core] of the work I do as a university professor.[48]

A member of the UNC Press board explained: "Everyone knew it was wrong, but we also knew the harder we fought, the more damage the Board of Governors could do to the Press.... They have shown a willingness to go after people who oppose them time and again."[49] The press feared that the Board of Governors would intervene even more outrageously, "trying to manage which books it publishes and why." It was better, perhaps, not to "poke the bear." For its part, the Board of Governors simply maintained its steely silence. Arbitrary power need not explain itself. Campus and system administrators offered their by-then-habitualized silent and submissive obedience. One of the nation's great university presses was thus notably harmed, and an intended message once again had been dramatically delivered to Carolina faculty and staff. Eric Muller is a rare academic of brilliance, generosity, and courage. The UNC Board of Governors made it clear that particular combination is no longer to be tolerated at the University of North Carolina.[50]

Around the same time, the UNC Board of Trustees opted to do its partisan duty and famously entered the fray. And, to be candid, they were notably more ambitious. It's one thing to attack some centers from a law school or express a usurping disdain for an academic press, but in 2021, the UNC–Chapel Hill Board of Trustees moved to block the tenure of famed journalist and alumna Nikole Hannah-Jones. Giving the back of the hand to Carolina's storied journalism school, the trustees decided that Hannah-Jones, winner of a Pulitzer Prize, receiver of a MacArthur Foundation "Genius Grant," inductee into the NC Media & Journalism Hall of Fame, and African American director of what is likely the most notable public history project ever launched, wasn't up to Republican snuff. A trustee named Chuck Duckett—who works for a marketing services firm whose website explains it "provides packaging solutions to innovative craft beer and wine/spirits companies"—had reservations about Hannah-Jones's scholarly attainment.[51] Duckett was apparently unimpressed with journalism school dean Susan King's assessment that Hannah-Jones's tenure package was "the best" she had ever seen.[52]

The decision was met with universal, even international, derision. The *New York Times*, *Washington Post*, and *London Guardian* ran extensive, damning stories on the triumph of politics and racism over academic integrity at UNC. The *Chronicle of Higher Education* published a piece, landing in the inbox of every academic administrator in the country, headlined, "The Tenure Denial of Nikole Hannah-Jones Is Craven and Dangerous." UNC had thus completed its massive rebranding exercise of the last decade—going from being perceived as one of the nation's most respected public universities to a right-wing, racial-equality-denying, politically interventionist clown car.

Board of Trustees chairman Richard Stevens made a cowardly attempt to shift the blame for the decision to the journalism dean. The perpetually civil chair of the UNC–Chapel Hill faculty assembly, Mimi Chapman, was forced to explain that Stevens's statement was "de facto" false. Chancellor Guskiewicz went into his traditional crouch, avoiding comment and effectively going into hiding as his campus committed one of the most visible exercises of racial hiring discrimination in decades. Later, with the campus exploding, faculty of color departing, and the African American president of the student body warning minority applicants not to come to Chapel Hill because it was incapable of a "racial reckoning," Guskiewicz explained: "I support the academic freedom of our faculty; I also respect the role our Board of Trustees plays in our model of shared governance." Now there's some leadership. One would have thought Guskiewicz would have learned from his predecessor, Carol Folt, that with these overseers, even agreeing not to do your job doesn't mean you get to keep your job.

After months of intense turmoil, the Board of Trustees caved and belatedly voted to reverse itself, ratifying Hannah-Jones's tenure. She rejected the offer on live, national television, accepting instead a welcoming and far more generously endowed tenured position at Howard University. Professor Hannah-Jones explained that she could obviously have no confidence in her "ability to exert academic freedom" in Chapel Hill, and she refused to accept any appointment at a university "whose leadership permitted this conduct and has done nothing to disavow it."[53]

Chuck Duckett, Richard Stevens, and their trustee colleagues had neither the talents nor the inclination to actually judge Nikole Hannah-Jones's academic attainment and potential. They were interested, instead, in visibly endorsing North Carolina Republicans' latest cultural charade—the phantom and dishonestly generated threat of critical race studies. Professor Hannah-Jones's *New York Times* "1619 Project" had become a flashpoint in the national effort to circumscribe teaching about racism in

U.S. society and history. Right-wing columnists from the hilariously entitled and Art Pope–funded James G. Martin Center for Academic Renewal had warned feverishly against her appointment. Two Republican U.S. representatives, Virginia Foxx and Greg Murphy, demanded that the chancellor block the hire, complaining of Hannah-Jones's "portrayal of white America."[54] The UNC–Chapel Hill Board of Trustees successfully showed the world that they, too, despite their sworn statutory duties, were happy to act merely as an instructed caucus of the North Carolina Republican Party. No plainer statement could be made that Howard Odum's charge "to expose the facts, encourage reform, smooth social change, and make democracy effective in the unequal places" was no longer to hold sway at the University of North Carolina.

The Demand for Submissive Leaders

In 2015, UNC president Tom Ross was fired by the Board of Governors for not being a Republican. They didn't stop there. His successor, Margaret Spellings, was hired for her notable Republican political credentials. Her presidency, though, lasted less than two years—either, it is reported, because she was "insufficiently conservative for the Board of Governors' taste or unwilling to do its bidding."[55] Peter Hans, who had no university employment experience whatsoever, was hired in 2020 without significant faculty input, formal or informal, into the process.[56] He was, though, praised for his close relationship to North Carolina Republican legislators; by then, seemingly, it was the only credential that mattered. The high presidential turnover rate and the bold selection linkage to partisan affiliation led the American Association of University Professors to state the obvious in its study of UNC: "only someone who will not challenge the agenda and interests of the [North Carolina Republican] legislature working through the Board of Governors will be considered for the position of UNC president."[57]

Nor have high-level Chapel Hill administrators escaped the demand for ideological conformity. Carol Folt, a UNC chancellor who was famed for never taking a position on anything, was fired in 2019 for annoying the

Board of Governors through her handling, or nonhandling, of the Silent Sam Confederate war monument controversy.[58] Folt's successor, Kevin Guskiewicz, has been forced to humiliate himself before Republican-demanded orthodoxies both during his candidacy and after accepting appointment. It deeply wounds a historic institution and its members to witness its purported leader grovel in dishonest submission in order to hold on to a now shamed and pitiful academic position. The unexpressed perpetual excuse, "If I stood up for principle and protected the essential values of the university, then they would only fire me and get someone even worse," may well be true. But it is also, undoubtedly, the excuse that forgives all transgressions—every single one.[59]

In December 2021, professor Christopher Clemens, a self-described "outspoken conservative" on the UNC faculty, was named the provost by the UNC–Chapel Hill Board of Trustees after a search process "fraught with allegations of outside political interference."[60] UNC faculty chair Mimi Chapman published a chastising op-ed in the *Daily Tar Heel* just before Clemens's selection, describing a heavily orchestrated pressure campaign from Republican overseers: "Our trustees and the UNC system are dictating [the chancellor's] choices to the point that he really has none to make." Chapman explained that faculty members, going forward, will "need to think carefully before participating in an upper-level search at UNC unless we are comfortable with our dedication to a meaningful process being made only for show."[61] Clemens's seemingly coerced appointment process has been mirrored on other UNC System campuses, including the Board of Governors hiring its own utterly unqualified members for crucial campus administrative positions.[62]

Peter Hans's first act as UNC president was to formally institutionalize the outside intrusion. Hans and the Board of Governors adopted a "highly unorthodox" new process to search for chancellors.[63] Under the change—which was apparently previously unknown in public higher education—the system president gained the unilateral authority to add to the applicant pool two candidates who are unapproved by the campus search committee. One of the two "stranger" candidates then must be deemed a "finalist" in the search and is to be recommended to the president and the Board of Governors. The feint neatly removes shared faculty governance from the selection process. By choosing one of his automatic finalists, the president is thus empowered to select a chancellor for each campus in the system who has been completely rejected as unsuitable by the institution's faculty and administrative leadership. The pathway to the uninhibited selection of Republican hacks with no qualifications except an undying fealty to their political benefactors is thereby ensured. The University of North Carolina at Chapel Hill has been long regarded as one of the four or five best public universities in the United States. Oddly, it can now be completely excluded from the selection of its leader. That determination is to be made solely by the Republican leadership of the General Assembly through its water carriers on the UNC Board of Governors. The political occupation is thus rendered complete.

The impact of this newly created regime of dominance is difficult to calculate. Faculty and students, of course, depart. No qualified and nationally competitive academic leader would even consider applying for a job under such perils because, by definition, they would be prevented from actually undertaking their formerly independent responsibilities. And, of course, any hired leaders might well be dispatched on a political whim, as their predecessors have been. So the pool of potential leadership candidates becomes grotesquely thin, warped, and diminished. It is inevitably limited to those who do not prize, and will not be committed to enforce, the foundational values of American public universities. It requires candidates who are willing to agree not to actually do their jobs in order to keep their jobs—as if great public universities could thrive under the faux leadership of cowards, partisan hacks, and sycophants. The legacy of Frank Graham, Bill Friday, Bill Aycock, and Julius Chambers has thus been successfully interred.

Killing the Goose

The political assault on the University of North Carolina violates traditional norms of academic freedom, independence, and rigor. It also blocks and impedes crucial racial reckoning and progress. To highlight the point,

in the summer of 2022, the famed journalism school in Chapel Hill had
its accreditation downgraded, and the American Association of University
Professors found that the UNC System had repeatedly violated academic norms and standards of racial equality through wounding and corrosive outside political interference. The transgressions, outside reviewers
concluded, crush the quality and the meaning of the university. They constitute, as well, bold usurpations of governing authority. But there's more
than that. They're also stupid.[64]

The UNC Board of Governors, their benefactors in the General Assembly, and their toadies on the Board of Trustees believe that they can
run scholars out because they don't like what they say and replace world-class faculty and administrators with utterly unqualified Republicans
and UNC will remain one of the nation's most prestigious institutions.
Board of Governors members might even swap coveted leadership positions among themselves or their buddies in the statehouse. Nice salaries
and easy work, the theory seems to go. But the American academy doesn't
work that way. Competition is intense and unyielding. Faculty and students simply turn to more appealing vineyards, and after a decade of political pummeling, UNC is no longer UNC. It is notably wounded. Still,
I can personally attest that North Carolina lawmakers, like so many other
Tar Heels, are often frantic for their own children be admitted to a great,
distinguished, and immensely lauded public university. When they are
finished with their pillaging, it won't be there anymore.

And the phenomenon isn't limited to North Carolina. As the *Chronicle of Higher Education* has put it:

> Colleges have been drawn into the red-hot center of America's raging culture wars. And as higher education is attacked as an institution, employees up and down the ladder find their professional lives
> more difficult. Faculty members at state institutions feel under siege.
> Politically appointed governing boards examine what they can teach,
> research and write. Presidents, especially at public colleges, are in the
> hot seat. The caustic political climate risks reshaping and disrupting
> the career paths of young and seasoned academics alike. Some will

think twice about applying for jobs at certain institutions, while others decamp for greener, less partisan pastures. And there is a partisan geography to higher education's current clashes.[65]

The implications of this "geography" are immensely troubling. "Public flagships in red states" can find themselves "at a disadvantage compared with their peers in blue states or in private universities," the *Chronicle* notes. Red-state public universities will struggle to maintain academic prestige. Michael Harris, a professor of higher education and the chair of educational policy at Southern Methodist University, says, "It feels like we could have two separate systems, one red and one blue."[66] Yet again, I fear, North Carolina leads the way downward.[67]

Lux Libertas

Democratic governance demands the piercing eye of a questioning populace. And an empowered and participatory citizenry begins with the independent explorations of dramatically engaged students—young and old. Public universities are meant, our forebears have thought, to be special laboratories for the understanding and critique of our social order as well. This has meant, scholars have suggested, that when the university fulfills its mission, it triggers social improvement and public response.[68]

William Aycock, who was UNC's chancellor in the 1950s and '60s, argued—in the face of threatened legislative interference—that UNC's mission embraces "the duty to examine the bases, foundations, and assumptions upon which present knowledge" and institutional arrangements rest. The university itself, Aycock claimed, was "fathered in rebellion against oppression and mothered by a vision of freedom. It has become an instrument of democracy and a place in which the weak can go strong and the strong can go great."[69]

One of Aycock's successors, James Moeser (2000–2008), thought that UNC's long history revealed an obligation for "the university to hold contemporary culture up to the critical light in the context of freedom," citing the motto: *lux libertas* ("light and liberty").[70] Noting the explicit leadership of Frank and Edward Kidder Graham, Bill Friday, and Bill Aycock, Moeser told his university colleagues:

> We have a moral responsibility to our state and our nation as a public university to bring to the public square the great issues of our day, without fear of censorship. Just as Chancellor Aycock and President Friday worked to defeat the repression of free speech embodied in the Speaker Ban and just as President [Frank Porter] Graham spoke out vehemently against the use of the atomic bomb, we must be willing to take a stand on critical issues of the day.... The university must have a moral compass. As I study the history of this place, that is the characteristic that shines through in our greatest moments. [The university] has been both a rock of stability and an agent of change.... [It has been, in Edward Kidder Graham's words] the instrument of democracy for realizing the high and healthy aspirations of the state.[71]

CHAPTER FIVE

Movement vs. Partisan Politics

We are dealing with one side that is undermining the very essence of
what it means to be a country that roots itself in this philosophy of equal
protection under the law. You cannot battle that if folks on the other side
are always moderating, modulating, and compromising.... You fight a
crisis until the crisis is over. You can't overreach when you're at
the bottom, and these folks have taken us to the bottom.
—Rev. Dr. William J. Barber II, co-chair of the Poor People's Campaign[1]

t is no exaggeration to claim that, over the last dozen years, the North
Carolina General Assembly has waged one of the stoutest wars
launched by any American state in the past half century against poor
people, people of color, the LGBTQ+ community, public education,
the environment, and even democracy itself.[2] State senate leader Ralph
Hise Jr. has often bragged of what he deems his Republican colleagues'
singular achievement: amassing the most relentlessly right-wing legacy of
any legislature in the nation.[3] Hise, no doubt, has done his part by unconstitutionally gerrymandering electoral districts, kicking hundreds of
thousands of qualifying poor kids off the food stamp rolls, giving millions
of public dollars to religious organizations to preach to vulnerable people that God doesn't want them to get an abortion,[4] and the like. But the
crusade to reject constitutional equality has been a broad-based, continuing, and relentlessly enthusiastic partisan project. As the *Atlantic* has explained, "Nowhere is the battle between liberal and conservative visions
of government—on the environment, on guns, on abortion, on campaign
finance, on religion, on taxes—fiercer than in North Carolina."[5] And, as

explained in the *New York Times*, there has "been a desperate effort" in the Tar Heel State to erase any trace of progressive decision-making:

> Republicans have operated as thieves in the night. They have targeted jobless benefits, education and welfare spending, while pushing for redistricting and limits on voting rights to keep themselves in power. The state finds itself in a situation that looks akin to the South of the 1890s.[6]

So, in one sense, it is unsurprising that the radicalized handiwork of the North Carolina General Assembly triggered a massive counter-campaign, a bold and inspired, almost desperate protest movement. Many Tar Heels had come to believe that the very character of their state was under shocking assault. The society they had long loved and embraced was threatened, almost daily, before their very eyes. With each new legislative session, restraints that had been previously unheard of were proffered and often enacted. Lawmakers didn't embark on a session or two "blowing-off-steam" adventure. The crusade was relentless, burgeoning, and unrelenting. Many thought the very nature of North Carolina society was hanging in the balance— and they were right to think so.

In April 2013, Rev. William J. Barber and about fifty supporters held the first of what they deemed "Moral Monday" demonstrations outside the North Carolina General Assembly building in Raleigh.[7] Seventeen people were arrested, as Reverend Barber put it, for "holding up pictures of the Constitution and scriptures from the Bible."[8] On the next Monday, those seventeen would expand to thirty-four. Then, thirty-four became sixty-eight. Crowds grew from hundreds to the tens of thousands—even, at the height of the protests, to one hundred thousand or more in downtown Raleigh.[9] Throughout the summer, as the rallies swelled, more than a thousand hearty souls were arrested for acts of civil disobedience.[10] Barber later explained:

> When you see something that's wrong, eventually you have to do something about it. We were a freedom family, doing what we had learned to do. We didn't know where it would lead, but we knew we

had to do everything in our power to expose the extremism that had become so normal in the daily news.[11]

Barber readily conceded that he "was surprised to see that hundreds of people had repeatedly showed up on Jones Street [at the General Assembly building] on only a few days' notice."[12] But soon, of course, the legislative building itself proved to be too small a venue. The "incredible thing," Barber noted, was that it "kept happening, over and over again." Gigantic crowds stood outside the statehouse for thirteen consecutive Mondays. The massive throngs were notably diverse. Marchers bellowed, "This is what democracy looks like." And, by God, it was.

But even if the Moral Monday protests seemed like spontaneous combustion, they weren't. With the help of an array of progressive ministers and social justice allies, Reverend Barber was elected president of the North Carolina NAACP in 2006.[13] He was adamant to immediately move the storied Tar Heel civil rights organization "beyond the banquets." Within a year, Barber had launched the Historic Thousands on Jones Street (HkonJ) movement, mobilizing not only 120 NC NAACP chapters, but more than 150 community, religious, labor, and social organizations around the state. In February 2007, an HkonJ "People's Assembly" developed and adopted a consensus-based, fourteen-point platform that formed the backbone of the extensive organizing efforts that were to follow. As HkonJ broadened its reach and its potent membership roster, it held annual mobilizations to challenge the (then-Democratic) General Assembly to address the needs and demands of the marginalized and excluded. Activism on behalf of the meaningful integration of public schools, much-needed labor-union-organizing campaigns, the massive poverty tour that I mentioned in chapter 2, and an array of surprisingly successful efforts in small and large communities across North Carolina quickly ensued. If Moral Mondays had produced an explosion, then the blast was rooted in years of intense and tireless grassroots field work.[14]

Maybe it is less surprising then that within two years of the first protests in Raleigh, Moral Monday movement coalitions had come together in fourteen states—not only in the South, but across the Midwest, New

York, and Maine[15]—or that, in May 2017, Reverend Barber, along with
Dr. Liz Theoharis of the Union Theological Society, announced that they
were taking the Moral Monday movement national, forming the Poor
People's Campaign, pressing "fusion politics," and aiming to unite people of all races and creeds in a fight for progress that was rooted in moral
rather than political terms. "The language of left versus right and liberal
versus conservative is too puny to challenge the extremism we're facing
now," Barber claimed.[16]

Movement Politics

It's not easy to describe the might and uplift of the Moral Monday protests. First, of course, there was their surprising and pervasive power.
Huge crowds in Raleigh, Charlotte, Greensboro, and Durham might be
one thing, but in Asheville, Goldsboro, Manteo, Salisbury, Rocky Mount,
Wilmington, and Burlington? Good Lord. Who would have guessed that
North Carolina would produce the largest civil rights protest in the South
since the Selma-to-Montgomery march of 1965?[17]

And then there was the remarkable and almost unmatched diversity
of the demonstrators. Because of the convening leadership of the North
Carolina NAACP, some assumed that the Moral Monday movement was
or would become a largely African American crusade. But given Reverend Barber's embracing and inclusive leadership, that was never likely, and
the boisterous statehouse rallies were, in fact, marvelously diverse: Black,
white, Latinx, Indigenous, gay, straight, trans, rural, urban, documented,
undocumented, activists, first-time participants, preachers, rabbis, working people, union members, teachers, students, homeless folks, professors,
mayors, judges, even some Republicans. And most stunning, to me at least,
was the demonstrators' age range. There were a lot of seniors, to be sure,
as is true of most political gatherings. (My favorite handmade sign, of the
many thousands, was carried by a smiling, white-haired lady in her eighties
that read: "I can't believe I'm still protesting this same shit.") But the young
protesters surprised everyone. College students, high schoolers, kids tag-
ging along with their families, there were tons of them—part Woodstock,

part March on Washington. North Carolinians of literally every stripe and pedigree rose up and fought back—and came back for more.

Reverend Barber's influence also ensured both a discipline and a structure for the gatherings. Nonviolent, civil, courteous disobedience was the touchstone of the protests, and Reverend Barber's speeches provided the main act. But music and ceremony marked the assemblies as well. They were partly politics, partly church, partly concert, and partly family reunion. Often the most joyous and comical part of the sessions saw middle-aged (or older) white folks like me trying to bust a move to Marvin Gaye or Al Green. Forgivably ridiculous—perhaps. In tougher moments, deeply inspiring singers like Yara Allen or Mary Williams would still the crowds, reminding me of a conversation I had years ago with Andrew Young, when I was a different kind of academic, about Fannie Lou Hamer. Young said that when they had faced dangerous protests with Dr. King and were sometimes frightened themselves, they would ask Hamer to sing in her powerful, stunning voice. Then they would decide, he said, "If she wasn't scared, we wouldn't be either."

It was one of the high honors of my life to speak at a lot of these magical gatherings. Even for an old hand, the thrill of addressing tens of thousands of committed citizens is unparalleled (surpassed, in my experience, only by being invited to talk to the UNC football team a time or two before the annual Duke game). The inevitable give and take of a massive, ultra-engaged crowd reminds that one's "speech" is, at best, a joint effort—that energized protesters are going to take the conversation where they want it to go. The ride was invariably something of a treasure, but my favorite spot at Moral Monday protests was never on the stage. I preferred to be about a hundred yards back, in the middle of the moving throng, soaking up the energy of the Tar Heels around me—yelling, singing, swaying, howling, locking arms, and locking fates. I came to look forward to the weekly sessions. To be, yet again, with sisters and brothers in the cause. Reverend Barber himself would later describe the phenomenon as "learning to stand together and proclaim the deepest values of our traditions, experiencing a revival like we'd never seen before, lifting us from where we were to higher ground."[18]

Democratic Politics

So there is, in my experience, much driving force in North Carolina move-ment politics. And I mean to speak here more broadly of what I think of as protest politics—referring not only to the Moral Monday movement, but also to bold, separate activism by North Carolina teachers, environ-mentalists, equality advocates, democracy reformers, and the like. Our streets are often filled by their potent and energizing efforts.

But like a lot of folks who are involved in these efforts, I'm also much engaged in a second, broader, more traditional attempt to effect policy change in the Tar Heel State—the North Carolina Democratic Party. Pragmatically speaking, it is almost impossible to think that any other platform offers as realistic an opportunity to dislodge the North Carolina Republican Party's crusade against the poor and the marginalized. If Tar Heels are to defeat this broad effort to repeal the twentieth century, it'll be done only by winning Democratic majorities in both houses of the Gen-eral Assembly. All hope, finally, must be lodged in that project, but as an often highly absorbed North Carolina Democrat, I worry that the party cannot always take full advantage of the gift of the state's strong move-ment politics.

For me, there are two principal reasons for Democrats' seeming inabil-ity to fully capture and deploy the strength of the state's protest politics. The first is structural—or nearly structural. There is a notable chasm be-tween Democratic politics and movement politics. Some of the separa-tion is decidedly intentional.

Reverend Barber, as the most important example of the distinction, has been adamant to build a moral movement, not a partisan one. To be clear, no North Carolinian has done more to energize, register, and inspire Tar Heels to go to the polls than Barber. But he has carefully shielded the HkonJ demonstrations and the Moral Monday protests from an infusion of Democratic Party politicization. He has, in my view, been wise to do so, but the demarcation is more dramatic than many understand.

Reverend Barber himself has written of this distinction. He's explained that "the platform for our fusion coalition was one from which poor and hurting people's voices could be heard."[19] Once the movement caught fire, however, "the politicians who spend millions of dollars to get their faces on TV couldn't wait to get in front of the cameras."[20] So "we told them our stage wasn't for them":

> I'll never forget one evening as a registered Republican and a registered Democrat were standing together, talking about how the legislature had cut off their unemployment benefits, I noticed a state legislator giving an interview to the press [at the side of the stage]. As soon as our unemployed brothers had finished, I stepped to the microphone and asked the whole crowd to help me shame the politician into taking his show somewhere else. Anyone was welcome to be part of Moral Mondays, but we gathered to hear from the people about how our state's extremism was affecting them.[21]

I had earlier seen the discipline firsthand. Near the end of the poverty tour that our small center had helped carry out with the North Carolina NAACP and others, Reverend Barber and I hosted a town meeting in Rocky Mount. Because of Barber's presence and the ample organizing efforts of Reuben Blackwell, a longtime local community leader, the crowd was large, five hundred or more. And, perhaps more important, most of those in attendance were actually low-income folks rather than civil servants, officeholders, or political activists. Seeing the opportunity, a Democratic House member, who was mounting a serious campaign for governor, came to the eastern North Carolina gathering. During the discussions, he and his staff moved up and down the aisles, shaking hands and passing out brochures, knowing, he assumed, a fruitful Democratic flock when he saw one. To my surprise, and certainly to the candidate's horror, Reverend Barber took to the microphone and unceremoniously kicked the ambitious gubernatorial candidate out of the town hall meeting with his staff members in tow. Frankly put, I'd never seen anything like it. It was precisely what should have been done, of course, but I would never have had the nerve. Barber didn't bat an eye. He just continued the discussions. The chastened candidate knew better than to question the mandate. As I said, Barber's crusade was meant to be a moral, not a partisan, one.

But I'm convinced there is an even larger reason for the ample gulf between protest and partisanship. As I mentioned, I do a good deal of work
within the North Carolina Democratic Party. I'm anything but averse to
it. I'm confident that it's essential to the state's future. Perhaps because of
my writings, I speak at a lot of Democratic functions and, more relevant,
I've been invited a number of times to meet with various iterations of the
Democratic caucuses of the North Carolina General Assembly.[22] The caucus is replete with capable, inspiring, and battle-hardened leaders. Some
are even heroes to me. But the substance and tenor of discussions with
caucus members typically departs from the discourse of protest. While
much of North Carolina—me included—believes that the very meaning
and character of the commonwealth is urgently imperiled, its legislative
representatives, the minority party included, often don't seem to act as if
that is the case.

Ironically, the political class can somehow appear less alarmed and
more complacent than many of the rest of us are. Democratic lawmakers' queries and expositions are regularly not only pragmatic, but principally defensive. Many express great worry over the fear of offense. Officials fret about what might be held against them rather than what is at
stake for the commonwealth. There is little or no discussion of the unfolding war that has been waged by their adversaries against poor people
and people of color, little talk of a pioneering campaign of bigotry or a
spirited race to the constitutional bottom. There is no evidence of an almost revolutionary rejection of traditional norms and egalitarian values,
no outrage over the Republican project of destroying the notion of an
America for all. Instead, political leaders seem to search for a poll-tested,
existentially modest issue or proposal on which to stake their electoral
fortunes. Campaigns frequently reflect the same tepid nature. For example, Democratic candidates will spend the bulk of their available resources
on a series of television ads saying, only, that they would support modest increases in spending for education. The implication being, almost,
that if their Republican adversaries had merely been willing to spend
2 percent more on the schools, the whole extant crusade to demolish the
Fourteenth Amendment in North Carolina would be unobjectionable.

Rather than carrying forward the bold banner of moral struggle that has been demanded by the times, they seem like timid incrementalists, unwilling to face the enormity of the challenges that have been pressed by their adversaries, leaving the war on democracy and equality unexplored, unaddressed, undebated, and, ultimately, uncontested. The discourse of the protest movement could not be further removed from the discourse of the caucus room. Each reflects and occupies massively different terrains, seemingly foreign to the other, rather than being essential, linked components of a shared and existentially crucial struggle for democracy.

To make the point more particularly, I recall repeated requests from a U.S. Senate candidate whom I liked and admired seeking help with what she deemed to be flagging support in the North Carolina "progressive" community. I tried to remind her, gingerly, that every night on television, her commercials explained that she was more moderate, more like the Republicans, than any other sitting member of the Senate. And, of course, if you believe you're in a life-and-death struggle for your children's future, the last thing you might want to hear is that your supposed standard-bearer is the effective soulmate of your adversary. Similarly, an otherwise strong gubernatorial candidate complained that students and people of color had supported Barack Obama in droves but seemed uninterested in what she believed to be her crucial campaign. But since she had earlier declared her commitment to make access to higher education virtually impossible for the children of undocumented Tar Heels, no amount of enthusiasm could be garnered among those who were fighting to embrace the marginalized. Merely claiming that "the Republicans will be worse"—though perhaps it is true—is not an energizing call to battle. A "choice between cancer and polio," as the Rolling Stones put it, hardly compels one to storm the ramparts.[23]

Another way to put the challenge, perhaps, is that Democratic politicians seem immune to, or at least strongly averse to, essential claims of moral compulsion. Drawing on a non–North Carolina illustration, in the spring of 2022, Michigan lawmaker Mallory McMorrow seemed to jolt the nation with a stirring speech from the state senate floor in Lansing. Apparently, a Republican colleague had sent a fund-raising email accusing McMorrow of wanting to indoctrinate critical race theory and to "groom and sexualize" children as the latest move in the harsh and dishonestly concocted culture war. McMorrow, who is a new legislator and the mother of a one-year-old, decided, unlike other Democratic members, to punch back. She rose to protest the "hollow, hateful scheme":

> So who am I? I am a straight, white, Christian, married, suburban mom who knows that the very notion that learning about slavery or redlining or systemic racism somehow means that children are being taught to feel bad about themselves because they are white is absolute nonsense. I want every child in this state to feel seen, heard, and supported, not marginalized because they are not straight, white, and Christian. We cannot let hateful people tell you otherwise to scapegoat and deflect from the fact that they're not doing anything to fix the real issues that impact people's lives. People who are different are not the reason that our roads are in bad shape or that health care costs are too high or that teachers are leaving the profession. And I know that hate will win only if people like me stand by and let it happen. We will not let hate win.[24]

McMorrow's speech quickly went viral—beyond viral. Grateful activists, who were frustrated that so few elected Democrats speak out powerfully against the constant Republican offensives against people of color and the LGBTQ+ community, lionized the courageous, angry, and immensely articulate Michigan state senator. President Joe Biden called to thank her for "saying a lot of what needed to be said" (and, of course, what he hadn't said). She received a quarter million dollars in unsolicited contributions in less than twenty-four hours—a stunning figure for a largely unknown state lawmaker. McMorrow "articulated what many people feel across the country," progressive theologian Jim Wallis claimed. "She's representing more people than she can even imagine."[25] The exhilaration, no doubt, came from the power of McMorrow's words. The surprise, though, arose because those unflinching words were uttered by an elected Democrat. We have yet to see a Mallory McMorrow in North Carolina.

The Largest Gulf

If the yawning separation between movement and partisan politics dimin-
ishes opportunities for social and economic progress in North Carolina,
then there is yet another polarization that is even more troublesome and
historically frustrating. A few years ago, I spent several months interview-
ing low-income Tar Heels in two very distinct communities, Goldsboro
and Wilkes County. Our studies there indicated, yet again, that North
Carolina's economic prospects are not widely shared. Both communities
fell on the unfortunate side of the state's imposing rural–metropolitan
divide. But the conversations also highlighted a continuing polarization
that rends the politics of North Carolina and the South.

Goldsboro lies about sixty miles southeast of Raleigh. Its population,
some thirty-six thousand people, has actually dropped since 1990. Although Seymour Johnson Air Force Base provides a sound and much-
needed economic foundation, Goldsboro's poverty challenges are among
the most daunting in North Carolina.[26]

A recent national study found Goldsboro to be one of the ten poorest
cities in America. Stanford University's mobility studies concluded that
95 percent of the country's metropolitan areas had better economic mobility rates than Goldsboro. The Pew Research Center determined that
the last decade had brought the city a 26 percent drop in median income
and huge losses in middle-income employment. Both figures were among
the worst in the country.[27]

About one-quarter of Goldsboro residents live in poverty. Almost
40 percent of all its kids are poor, and half of its African American children are. In some census tracts, 65 percent of Goldsboro's kids are impov-
erished, and it has nearly the worst racially driven, concentrated poverty
in North Carolina.

Safe, affordable housing is a gigantic problem. One full-time-working,
single mom's story is typical. All she can afford is the local housing authority, "and it's terrible and dangerous. There are gunshots all the time,"
she told me. "Ambulances and police are always here," she said. She wishes
there were "a porch or backyard where her children could play safely, but

that's not possible." The public school bus stops two blocks down the
street, but "everybody knows that's too dangerous for kids to walk to," she
sighed.[28]

Wilkes County shares much of this record of hardship, though it
wasn't always so. Nestled into the eastern slope of the Blue Ridge Mountains with the Yadkin River at its core, Wilkes County is about a half-hour
drive from Boone and shares much of Boone's natural beauty. Once home
to Lowe's Home Improvement, Northwest Bank, Holly Farms, Carolina
Mirror, and North Wilkesboro Speedway, the county was ravaged by the
North American Free Trade Agreement (NAFTA).[29]

The median income dropped by nearly 30 percent over fifteen years.
In the late 1990s, the unemployment rate was a remarkable 2 percent.
A decade later, it had soared to more than 13 percent. Half of all Wilkes
County households make less than $30,000 per year. More than one-fifth
of Wilkes County's sixty-nine thousand residents—and one-quarter of
its kids—live in poverty. Twice as many people live in mobile homes as
the state average. Disability and overdose and addiction rates are high.
Almost 90 percent of the county's population is white. Tina Krause, executive director of Hospitality House of Northwest North Carolina, explained, "A lot of folks in the community I love have a lot of things to
unpack." But "I have a heart for them," Krause said, "they are, by God,
Wilkes County."[30]

Decent, safe housing is a challenge in Wilkes County, too. I think particularly of a family I interviewed in a small mobile home during a swel-
tering summer. The trailers in the mobile home park were ancient and
pressed in close proximity. Confederate flags and Trump signs were on
broad display. (There were none in the housing projects of Goldsboro.)
The windows were closed tight and covered with sheets—despite the
heat. Fans ran at full speed, pushing around the stifling air. The smell of
mold was potent, and kids played on their aunt and uncle's floor. The
adults were hopeful that the young ones would have a better shot at life
than they'd had.

There was little trace of Raleigh's or Charlotte's economic booms in
Goldsboro or Wilkes County. As one local leader explained, "A lot of folks

here have been on the losing end for a long time and feel like they've had the shit kicked out of them." They're "frantic for their children's future."[31]

It is illuminating to think of the discussions we had around kitchen tables in both the Goldsboro projects and the Wilkesboro mobile home lots. I have no doubt that these disparate residents consider themselves political and cultural adversaries, but their fears and aspirations followed nearly identical paths. In conversation, they indicated that they seek better schools, higher-paying jobs, affordable housing, health care, and child care. They wanted safe streets, decent neighborhoods, electric bills that they could manage, and meaningful access to public transportation. They were also certain that their political leaders know absolutely nothing about their actual lives.[32]

The largest polarization in North Carolina politics, I'd guess, arises between these poor white voters and poor Black ones. But their needs and assumptions, their worries and challenges, end up sounding remarkably similar. If any political party or leader could help these two boldly divided camps realize how much they actually have in common, rather than continuing to ply their assumed and historic differences, our electoral prospects and fortunes could be radically transformed. This is, of course, the framing challenge of the American South—announced and decried from W. J. Cash's *The Mind of the South* to Bob Dylan's "Only a Pawn in Their Game."[33] If this divide could be bridged, then the bottom 50 percent in North Carolina might, at long last, secure the political representation and power that they deserve.

★ ★ ★

CHAPTER SIX

The Limits of Law

I went to college at Oklahoma State University, where I was a football player and philosophy major. I don't know if it's true, but the athletic department at OSU told me that I was the only football player in history to be a philosophy major. I mention this to make a different point. After I graduated, when I started law school at Texas, I didn't like it much. Property, contracts, torts, procedure—it seemed to me the unexamined life. That was true until the second semester, when I took constitutional law. That was something worth getting your arms around.

Americans have worked many of our largest questions of national meaning into the operation of constitutional law. What binds us as a people? What matters do we actually pledge our allegiance to? What do Americans owe to one another? What, on the other hand, do we reserve to ourselves and our private institutions? What do aspirational norms of liberty and equality actually entail? Do they change over time, or are they somehow set, finally, in time? Does the constitutional arc of our long-enduring political universe bend toward justice? How do we safeguard the barriers that we jointly proclaim to secure? What, ultimately, is the relationship between democracy and constitutionalism? No small matters these. Many of our most compelling, foundational social challenges end up forming the framework of our constitutional jurisprudence.

I was also surprised to learn, in 1973, that it was an interesting time to study constitutional law. Less than two decades earlier, the United States Supreme Court had decided the landmark case *Brown v. Board of Education*.[1] In a sense, that decision raised the high court from something of a deep and unsuccessful slumber. No longer would the justices relegate the

Constitution's most fundamental promises to obvious hypocrisy. No longer would the command of equal justice trigger only national and international shame. No longer would the American Constitution be interpreted as void and vacuous, unworthy of its status as the world's oldest written charter.

A stunning series of landmark rulings quickly followed *Brown*. Not only were other instances of racial discrimination invalidated, but sex and alienage classifications were called into question as well.[2] The Bill of Rights was effectively incorporated against the states.[3] Rights to vote and electoral representation received dramatically elevated protection.[4] The first amendment's free speech and press guarantees were massively invigorated.[5] The Establishment and Free Exercise Clauses were made rigorously enforceable.[6] A newly developed constitutional right to travel was recognized.[7] Procedural due process rights were dusted off and significantly expanded.[8] The reach of the state action doctrine was markedly and aggressively altered.[9] A new non-textual right to privacy was announced.[10] *Miranda v. Arizona, Roe v. Wade*, and *University of California v. Bakke* were handed down.[11] A constitutional revolution literally erupted.

But if the agenda of former Supreme Court justices Earl Warren, Thurgood Marshall, and William Brennan Jr. proved to be active and energetic, it was not without at least something of a philosophical mooring and consistency. Strong scholars such as John Hart Ely described the Warren Court approach as a "representation-reinforcing theory of judicial review." It was foundationally procedural in character, supporting the underlying premises of representative government rather than supplanting them. It sought to ensure that processes protecting individuals were scrupulously secured, but as important, it was designed to make certain that the broader political processes were kept functionally open and that American society's "habitual unequals" were treated fairly.[12] The court sought to press a coherent theory of representative government, clearing the channels of political change and correcting against certain types of discrimination that had been inflicted upon excluded minorities. Ely thought this approach provided a necessary enhancement and safeguarding of representative democracy and involved judges in tasks that they were better qualified to perform than political officials. It wasn't a simple usurpation of government by judiciary. Rather, the justices aimed to provide an essential policing of the political process to prevent existing holders of power from obstructing its operation in service of a status quo or their own entrenchment. They also recognized dangers inherent in representative democracy and sought to prevent government from withholding from various minorities the protection that it afforded to the majority.[13]

To what was surely no one's great surprise, the assumption by judges of a potent and society-altering role in the protection of equality and minority access triggered a potent, pervasive, and near-perpetual political backlash. Republican political candidates, high and low, for more than a half century, have campaigned enthusiastically against the allegedly wayward, activist justices of the United States Supreme Court. School prayer and integration decisions, opinions protecting newly declared rights of criminal defendants, affirmative action rulings, and—perhaps most virulently—abortion cases provoked dissenters' ire.

At bottom, our federal system of judicial review is a political one, dependent on the appointing and confirming participation of lawmakers and presidents. Since 1968, all three chief justices and thirteen of seventeen associate justices appointed to the United States Supreme Court have been Republicans—with either declared or tacit missions to dismantle their predecessors' legacy. Almost all announce, in now-cynical confirmation hearings, a commitment to precedent, to the rule of law, to merely calling the balls and strikes in a neutral fashion, and to enforcing the law as written rather than imposing their own ideological predispositions.

Apparently, none actually mean it. The result, in 2022, is a United States Supreme Court that is more activist and more partisan than any of its earlier iterations. But its activism, as I'll explain later in this chapter, is deployed in service of a decidedly different and dramatically undemocratic and marginalizing set of political values and preferences. It enlists the high court in direct opposition to the achievement of the American promise.

But even as national politics has worked to demean the mission and meaning of the United States Supreme Court, North Carolina has become an illuminating test laboratory, demonstrating how essential it is, in a successful democracy, to maintain an independent judiciary that is designed to protect the operation of representative government by "clearing the channels of political change and assuring the full and effective participation of excluded minorities."[14] Democracy can't endure, in other words, without robust guardrails—not so long as human beings constitute the ruling majority.

Judicial Review, a Lawless Legislature, and the Essential Role of Constitutional Law

The North Carolina General Assembly, which has been governed by large Republican majorities over the past decade, has been exceedingly bold in its efforts to enlarge and entrench its already-ample powers. It has delivered the most ambitious racial and political gerrymanders ever seen in the United States. It has openly announced that it drew new electoral maps in order to slant the playing field as much as humanly possible toward Republicans because they were considered more worthy rulers than Democrats. Republican lawmakers have made it harder for Black Tar Heels to vote in order to weaken their electoral prospects. They have effectively overturned local elections when their opponents prevailed. They have attempted to stack the state courts and dramatically limit the powers of the governor and attorney general when their opponents were elected to those positions. They've often lied about their purposes when seeking to pull off these efforts.[15]

Reviewing courts, usually federal ones, have thwarted many of these power-grabbing campaigns. The General Assembly has claimed, each and every time, that the judicial veto of its enactments constitutes impermissible usurpation because they say that the lawmakers—and only the lawmakers—exercise authority granted by the people. Some limits on legislative prerogative, however, inhere in constitutional democracy. To make the point simplistically, a state legislature may well be able to enact a law saying it is satisfied with its present makeup, so its members will no longer be required to stand for reelection; but in doing so, it would no longer be part of a functioning democracy. Having been a student of constitutional law for fifty years, I feel confident in declaring that the language that has been employed by reviewing courts in invalidating North Carolina legislative adventurism has been unusually pointed. It helps paint a picture of—and reveal the undeniable necessity of—independent judicial review to enforce the safeguards of democracy in free government. I'll supply a few examples.

One of the first sets of state legislative districts adopted by the Republican North Carolina General Assembly when it came to power was invalidated by a three-judge reviewing federal court as a rank exercise in racial discrimination. A "state-wide numerical target based on race" led to these districts, the judges ruled, not "traditional race-neutral principles like compactness, contiguity and respect for political subdivisions." All such neutral notions "were subordinated to race." Speaking with unusual candor, the judges went further: "Our holding is . . . attributable to the explicit and undisputed methods that the General Assembly employed in the construction of these districts."[16] As a result of lawmakers' instruction,

> All 28 districts challenged were racial gerrymanders constituting direct constitutional violations working substantial and continuing injuries [to the rights of equal political participation]. Plaintiffs and thousands of other North Carolina citizens have suffered severe constitutional harms stemming from the [lawmakers'] creation of racially gerrymandered districts in violation of the Constitution. These citizens are entitled to swift and effective relief. Therefore, we order the North Carolina General Assembly to draw remedial districts in their next legislative session to correct the constitutional deficiencies [that they created] in the Enacted Plans.[17]

A year later, in *Covington II*, the courts were forced to further explore a meaningful remedy for the constitutional transgression. "Almost six years after these districts were initially put in place and [then] found unconstitutional—during which North Carolina has conducted three primaries and three general elections using racially discriminatory districting plans," the General Assembly still contested meaningful relief.[18] Judge James

Wynn wrote that "the widespread, serious, and longstanding nature of the constitutional violation—among the largest racial gerrymanders ever encountered by a federal court—counseled in favor of granting the Plaintiffs' request." He noted, candidly,

> The legislative defendants have acted in ways that indicate they are more interested in delay than they are in correcting this serious constitutional violation.... As long as ours is a representative form of government, and our legislatures are those instruments of government elected by and directly representative of the people, the right to elect legislators in a free and unimpaired fashion is a bedrock of our political system.[19]

Then, Wynn took the gloves off.

> Defendants [argue] against ordering a special election because "the constitutional violation, at a minimum, is certainly subject to rational disagreement." That is patently wrong. There is no "rational disagreement" as to whether the districting plans at issue in this case violate the Constitution. The Supreme Court affirmed that conclusion without argument and without dissent. There is no disagreement between this Court and the Supreme Court's conclusion that the challenged districts are unconstitutional racial gerrymanders.[20]

Nor would Wynn give credence to the General Assembly's odd argument that the constitutional violations were, in effect, "too big to remedy." That theory, Wynn chided, would "provide a perverse incentive to state legislatures that choose to engage in unjustified race-based districting to do so as pervasively as possible so as to insulate their plans from effective judicial relief."[21]

Finally, the impatient and by now near-belligerent jurist cut to the foundational chase:

> The [extraordinary] scope of the constitutional violation at issue—unjustifiably relying on race to draw lines for legislative districts encompassing the vast majority of the state's voters—also means that

the districting plans intrude on popular sovereignty ... because the vote is both the mechanism through which people delegate their sovereignty to elected officials and the mechanism by which the people ensure that elected officials "have an habitual recollection of their dependence on the people."[22]

I've been reading federal constitutional cases for five decades. I've never seen a judge say anything like that.

Finally, there's the language of the federal court holding the North Carolina General Assembly's subsequent extreme political gerrymanders unconstitutional. Lawmakers, the court found, drew a plan to purposefully subordinate the interests of non-Republican voters "not because they believed doing so advanced any democratic, constitutional or public interest, but because they thought electing Republicans is better than electing Democrats."[23] As a result, the goal of the candidly named "Partisan Advantage" plan was to "minimize the number of districts in which Democrats would have the opportunity to elect a Democratic candidate." The federal judges, by now, had lost all patience with the General Assembly's self-aggrandizing and democracy-defacing lawlessness:

> In *Covington* the Supreme Court held that ... [the enacted] state legislative districts carried forward the racial gerrymandering that rendered the original versions of the districts unconstitutional, raising legitimate questions regarding the General Assembly's capacity or willingness to draw constitutional remedial districts. During the intervening months, [lawmakers] enacted a number of pieces of election-related legislation that federal and state courts have struck down as unconstitutional, ... further calling into question the General Assembly's commitment to enacting constitutionally compliant, nondiscriminatory election laws. Most significantly, additional time has passed. We continue to lament that North Carolina voters now have been deprived of a constitutional congressional districting plan—and, therefore, constitutional representation in Congress—for years. ... The "eleventh hour" is upon us, if indeed it has not already passed.[24]

Demonstrating, rather explicitly, the importance of independent federal judicial review when confronting a power-obsessed, partisan-riven legislature—at least by contrast—during this same time period, the Republican-dominated, elected North Carolina Supreme Court rejected similar constitutional challenges to the state's redistricting outrages. In an opinion by Justice (now Chief Justice) Paul Newby, the state court ruled, quietly, that

> redistricting in North Carolina is an inherently political and intensely partisan process that results in political winners and, of course, political losers. Political losses and partisan disadvantage are not the proper subject for judicial review. . . . Rather, the role of the court in the redistricting process is to ensure that North Carolinians' constitutional rights—not their political rights or preferences—are secure.[25]

In other words, Newby declared that Tar Heels have a lot of rights, but living in a democracy isn't one of them.

Judicial Review in the Service of Privilege

It is somewhat odd, I concede, to talk in such detail about a series of decisions that invalidate the North Carolina legislature's redistricting efforts. But I do so for two reasons.

First, *Covington I* and *II* and *Rucho*, the initial political gerrymandering case, starkly show the utter necessity for independent judicial review to "open the channels" of democracy, thereby protecting our "underlying premises of representative government."[26] The North Carolina General Assembly, by its repeated and almost unembarrassed line-drawing schemes (and biased voter identification requirements), has sought time and again to exclude African Americans from effective participation in the political process. Lawmakers repeatedly opted to favor their own ascendancy over defining democratic and egalitarian norms. And North Carolina Republican political gerrymandering plans were so singularly extreme that judicial acceptance of them would concede that politicians could simply legislate their own perpetual dominance. In other words, it's not possible—in either the short or long term—to sustain a democratic form of government under the suffocating control of such measures. Judges have to act, or the Constitution fails.

My second reason for focusing on these essential representation-reenforcing rulings is more distressing and less apparent: they may not be long for this world. On the particular front of voting rights, the Roberts Court has already dealt deadly blows. In two major and hugely controversial decisions, *Shelby County v. Holder* and *Brnovich v. Democratic National Committee*, the high court's Republican majority has voted, with a seeming nonchalance, to literally gut the landmark Voting Rights Act of 1965.[27] The ideology-driven justices cast aside decades of Supreme Court precedent without even the pretense of justification. As Justice Elena Kagan wrote in a blistering *Brnovich* dissent, "Never before has a statute done more to advance the nation's highest ideals . . . yet in the last decade this Court has treated no statute worse."[28] And, more directly, in *Rucho v. Common Cause*, Chief Justice John Roberts Jr. wrote an opinion for his Republican colleagues holding that political gerrymandering cases can't be entertained in the federal courts.[29]

Rucho, of course, didn't stop state courts from invalidating political gerrymanders under their own constitutions—as North Carolina and some other jurisdictions have readily done.[30] But these two lines of cases demonstrate a new willingness to use the authority of the United States Supreme Court to assist Republican lawmakers in closing off the channels of democracy, using entrenched power to place a heavy, white, ideological thumb on the already-unequal scales of electoral participation—representation reinforcement be damned. And the fact that the United States Supreme Court has accepted jurisdiction in a new North Carolina case (2023) seeking to limit the power of state courts to review various voting rights cases is decidedly ominous.[31] As the Brennan Center for Justice has explained, it can't be overstated "how radical and consequential this could be—no one other than Congress would be allowed to rein in the abuses of state legislatures."[32]

And redistricting cases are merely the tip of a much larger and even more revolutionary iceberg. With almost 80 percent of the Supreme

Court appointments since 1970, and especially with the three Trump selections—Neil Gorsuch, Brett Kavanaugh, and Amy Coney Barrett—Republican presidents have secured a dramatic and likely long-lived ideological transformation of the United States Supreme Court. Its present partisan split is a daunting 6–3, and age (which is always relevant to the makeup of the tribunal) remains on the side of the GOP. Clarence Thomas and Samuel Alito Jr., along with Gorsuch, Kavanaugh, and Barrett, are enthusiastic and unapologetic ideological activists in ways that Democratic nominees never seem to manage or, perhaps, aspire to. Chief Justice Roberts pursues exactly the same ideological path, though at a more leisurely and institution-oriented pace. The nation is in for a tough, enduring, heavily partisan, and anti-democratic ride.

And the altered judicial landscape has been accomplished under something of a false-flag operation. First, Republican nominees have expressed, disingenuously, a faithful and committed dedication to principles of stare decisis and the rule of law in their required Senate hearings in order to assure the nation that they are, in fact, independent jurists and not political henchmen. In almost every instance, the pious declarations have been knowingly untrue—offered like some empty ritual dance that the occasion demands.

Brett Kavanaugh's disturbing 2018 confirmation hearing presented perhaps the most nauseating example. Kavanaugh told the committee and the nation that he regarded *Roe v. Wade*, the 1973 abortion decision, as "settled precedent of the Supreme Court." Not only that, he continued, "but one of the most important things to keep in mind about *Roe* is that it has been reaffirmed many times over the past 45 years—most pointedly in *Planned Parenthood* in 1992." It is "precedent on precedent," he announced.[33] It turned out, of course, that Kavanaugh's pompous ode to precedent was a charade.[34] He moved to overrule *Roe* the first time he got the chance[35]—as he undoubtedly knew he would when he spoke before the committee.

There is a second, enduring component of the false flag that is even more distressing. Preferred Republican justices, following the purported lead of former justice Antonin Scalia, relentlessly and mind-numbingly explain that they consider themselves to be tied to the Constitution's text and history. Scalia announced, time and again, that "a rule of law that binds neither by text nor by any particular, identifiable tradition, is no rule of law at all."[36] Only by clinging to the framers' understood historical meaning of the constitution's vague and open-ended phrases can judicial review avoid usurping government via unmoored, life-tenured jurists, the theory goes.

This is purportedly the central tenet of Republican-driven constitutional adjudication. A Pew Research Center study found that 75 percent of Republicans, and only 23 percent of Democrats, assert that the United States Supreme Court should make its rulings "based on its understanding of what the Constitution meant as it was originally written."[37] "Original understanding" is the most oft-repeated commitment in Supreme Court hearings and federal political campaigns. It is the Republican tie that binds—except, of course, when it doesn't.

I don't want to make a treatise out of this. But think of the centerpieces of the Roberts and Rehnquist Courts' constitutional jurisprudence. Scalia favorites. No originalist could conceivably defend the *Citizens United* case, which provided aggressive First Amendment protection for endless corporate spending in elections.[38] The framers of the First Amendment didn't think of money as speech or corporations as constitutional persons. It is enough, perhaps, to recall Thomas Jefferson's notably declared wish: "I hope we shall crush in its birth the aristocracy of our moneyed corporations, which dare already to challenge our government to a trial of strength and bid defiance to the laws of our country."[39]

But today's Republican justices are committed to economic dominance of politics, as are their Republican political benefactors. And apparently, that's what matters, not original meaning. It's the politics, not the history. The *Heller* case, the beloved and unyielding font of Republican-claimed gun rights, casts aside both the text and history of the Second Amendment.[40] Nor does the new *Bruen* gun case pass originalist muster.[41] But Scalia didn't let that get in his way. Scalia's historical and heuristic skills could be occult when the occasion demanded. The same can be said of his famous opinion in *Printz v. United States*, which invalidated an essential component of the Brady Handgun Violence Prevention Act.[42] There Scalia could find not a shred of either constitutional text or historical practice to justify throwing out the congressionally enacted gun-control measure. No worries, his politics were aroused. So were those of his "conservative," "originalist" colleagues. A little flexibility is called for, in other words, to carry out the Republican Party agenda under the fraudulent auspices of constitutional adjudication. And Scalia was nothing if not flexible.

My favorite example of originalist adventurism concerns affirmative action. Former justice Scalia and his colleagues were (and are) beyond adamant that it is unconstitutional for the federal government to use race as a classifier in affirmative action programs.[43] In fact, in the Supreme Court's principal case restricting federal affirmative action, Scalia wrote a separate opinion—while concurring in the majority offering—to make it clear that such affirmative action "can never" be justified in our constitutional order.[44]

Now, don't get me wrong; I understand that there are a lot of reasons why one could object to affirmative action. I'm convinced, given our brutal and bloody history, that modest steps to effectively and meaningfully integrate this still-opportunity-divided society are essential, but I know that many disagree. What I don't understand, however, is how a constitutional originalist can come to the conclusion that the use of affirmative action by the federal government is unconstitutional.

First, there is, simply put, no text on which to hang one's hat. The Fourteenth Amendment's Equal Protection Clause applies only to the states, not the federal government. And if we're to venture beyond the text, what extant legal tradition of equality, which was so pervasive in 1789 in the United States, could be identified and now enforced against the federal government? We embraced, at the country's founding, slavery, three-fifths–humanity status, the legal disenfranchisement and denied personhood of women, discrimination against non-Protestant religionists, atheists, noncitizens, and so on. The list, as you know, is long—and enduring. So what vision of equality, afoot in 1789, arises to non-textually invalidate discrimination by the federal government against white folks in 2022? What renders it unconstitutional? Former justice Scalia didn't like it. It's lousy policy, he said. Not a word did he offer about original understanding. His theory couldn't be allowed to get in the way of his politics, so he simply ignored his professed, defining constraint. "Let's not talk about it," seemed to be the explanation. Federal affirmative action is unconstitutional because my friends and I oppose it. That was apparently good enough. A rule is not a rule if, utterly without explanation, you get to decide when you'll apply it and when you won't. That's what politicians do, not jurists.

Much more Republican originalist-discarding work could be highlighted: the odd, usurping trashing of the Voting Rights Act,[45] the court's expansive claims of regulatory taking,[46] its creation of a swarm of states' rights doctrines to thwart congressional power,[47] and its newly invented limits on the reach of the Commerce Clause.[48] These constitutional transgressions arise simply because Republicans don't approve of them. The constitution coincides, perfectly, with their political predilections. Who would guess?

So, in North Carolina, we know well the necessity of independent judicial review, and like the rest of the country, we presently witness its imminent constructive demise. We now enter a new frontier—exploring how profoundly the United States Supreme Court can crush American democracy in the service of right-wing, equality-suppressing, Republican politics. Overruling *Roe v. Wade* is merely the heralding.[49] In a single week in June 2022, the Republican United States Supreme Court ruled that the American concept of constitutional liberty protects guns but not a person's right to reproductive freedom.[50] And they did that while recognizing, one assumes, that huge majorities of the citizenry strongly disagree with them. These are not justices. This is not a court. The nation would be better served by shutting its doors.

Of course, this is not the first time in American history that our highest tribunal has donned these tragedy-laden robes. The United States Supreme Court, after all, gave us *Dred Scott v. Sandford*,[51] *Plessy v. Ferguson*,[52] *Lochner v. New York*,[53] *Buck v. Bell*,[54] *Korematsu v. United States*,[55] *San Antonio v. Rodriguez*,[56] *Bowers v. Hardwick*,[57] and *Buckley v. Valeo*[58] even before *Citizens United, Shelby County*, and *Dobbs*.[59] It is not unfair to say that the history of the U.S. Supreme Court, in the cause of human liberty, is a decidedly mixed one. The justices may well have inflicted more blows against the overarching progress of constitutional equality over the generations than for it. But if North Carolinians, and Americans more broadly, have thought of the Supreme Court in the past as an effective and reliable safeguard and guarantor of equal justice for all, then those days, tragically, are over.

Bayard Rustin's Counsel

In the summer of 2022, in Chapel Hill, we celebrated the seventy-fifth anniversary of the cases arising from the first freedom ride, the 1947 Journey of Reconciliation. Or, more precisely, the judicial rulings weren't celebrated; they were marked, and their horrors were noted. Our cadre of local judges professed to the outrages and apologized for the famed injustice.[60] In 1946, the United States Supreme Court had ruled that state segregation laws couldn't constitutionally be applied to interstate travel, but nothing had actually changed as a result. So the Congress of Racial Equality, prodded by Bayard Rustin and George Hauser, organized what we now think of as the first freedom ride, the 1947 Journey of Reconciliation, which was designed to test the enforcement of the Supreme Court's nondiscrimination declarations.

Moving across the Upper South—from Washington, D.C., to Nashville—the bus riders sought to avoid the terrors of Mississippi and Alabama. They stuck to supposedly more civilized places, like Frank Porter Graham's Chapel Hill. There, the sixteen male Black and white riders met the tour's greatest violence and most grotesque abuse by the legal system. So much for the southern part of heaven.

After comparatively uneventful stops in Richmond, Petersburg, Oxford, and Durham, a Trailways driver ordered the riders to the back of the bus in Chapel Hill and then, upon their refusal, successfully sought their arrest. A violent mob of Tar Heels then attacked the travelers, screaming hate-filled epithets for "coming down here to stir up the n___s." A local pastor tried to get the riders to the safety of his nearby parsonage, where other serious assaults occurred. UNC student volunteers eventually transported the riders by car to a rousing, supportive mass meeting at Shiloh Baptist Church in Greensboro so that the trip could continue.[61]

Cases against the freedom riders were dropped in Durham, Asheville, and Virginia, but not in Chapel Hill. Weeks later, several riders, including Bayard Rustin, were tried there and sentenced to thirty days on a horrifying chain gang in Roxboro, North Carolina. Rustin refused to appeal the decision to the United States Supreme Court, preferring to broadcast the outrage to the world. At the end of his abuse-laden and life-threatening sentence, Rustin walked out, head high, undaunted by his North Carolina tormentors.

Of course, Chapel Hill didn't have the final word. In 2013, then-president Barack Obama awarded Bayard Rustin a posthumous Presidential Medal of Freedom, praising his lifelong "march toward equality, regardless of who we are and who we love." UNC's fabled basketball coach Dean Smith was honored the same day.[62]

The Journey of Reconciliation was controversial even within the civil rights community. The great Thurgood Marshall was dead set against it, fearing it would "become a bloodbath." But Rustin pushed back: "Unjust social laws do not change because supreme courts deliver opinions. Social progress comes from struggle. All freedom demands a price. Courtroom arguments will not suffice for the rights today demands."[63]

As we enter a new era, with a lawless, rigidly politicized United States Supreme Court seeking to wage war against democracy and equality rather than support and sustain them, Rustin's words resonate—as powerful and necessary as they were seventy-five years ago.

CHAPTER SEVEN

Democracy, Equality, and the Future of America

"Four score and seven years ago," Abraham Lincoln declared, in the nation's most important public address, the United States was "conceived in liberty" and "dedicated to the proposition that all men are created equal."[1] Eighty-seven years was no accident. Lincoln found both America's origin and its mission in the Declaration of Independence. As the country's commander in chief, of course, he could have cited 1789, when the United States Constitution was initiated, and which the Civil War sought to rend, as the relevant marker. But Lincoln knew well the Constitution's compromises on slavery, democracy, and equality. And as the nation tore itself apart on the way to war, Lincoln argued that "on the question of liberty," we are not "what we once were." "Our republican robe has been soiled and trails in the dust," he noted.[2]

In responding to Stephen Douglas in their Senate election debates, Lincoln said:

> When we were the political slaves of King George and wanted to be free, we called the maxim that "all men are created equal" a "self-evident truth," but now when we have grown fat, and lost all dread of being slaves ourselves, we have become so greedy that we call the same maxim "a self-evident lie."[3]

Accordingly, the central theme of Lincoln's unsuccessful 1858 Senate campaign and later his presidency was that the nation should "re-adopt the Declaration of Independence, and the practices and policies which harmonize with it." Only by doing so would the Union be secured and "so saved as to make it worthy of the saving."[4]

To Lincoln, the "sentiment" of the Declaration "was that which gave promise that in due time the weights would be lifted from the shoulders of all." The noble experiment of self-government hung in the balance. "Most governments," he wrote, "have been based on the denial of the equal rights of men." Ours, on the other hand, "began by affirming those rights." He told his first Congress:

> This is essentially a people's contest. On the side of the Union it is a struggle for maintaining in the world that form and substance of government whose leading object is to elevate the condition of men—to lift artificial weights from all shoulders; to clear the paths of laudable pursuits for all. Yielding to partial and temporary departures from necessity, this is the leading object of the government for whose existence we contend.[5]

Lincoln did not ignore the contradictions of the Declaration. As Martin Luther King Jr. would remind us a century later, "that document was always a declaration of intent rather than of reality."[6] Slavery was only the most brutal and horrifying of its realities. In truth, of course, the "all" who were "created equal" were, at best, white, propertied, Protestant males. Lincoln claimed, though, that the authors of the Declaration "did not mean to assert the obvious untruth that all were then actually enjoying that equality, nor yet, that they were about to confer it immediately upon them":

> They meant simply to declare the right, so that enforcement of it might follow as circumstances should permit. They meant to set up a standard maxim for a free society, which could be familiar to all, and revered by all, constantly looked to, constantly labored for, and even though never perfectly attained, constantly approximated, thereby constantly spreading and deepening its influence.[7]

In Lincoln's view, our constitutive principles were more basic and profound than the specifics set forth in the U.S. Constitution. Framing an illustration based on biblical metaphor, he explained: "There is something back of the Constitution and the Union entwining itself more closely about the human heart . . . the principle of 'Liberty to all'—the principle that clears the path for all, gives hope to all and, by consequence, enterprise and industry to all."

> The expression of that principle in our Declaration of Independence was the word "fitly spoken" which has proved an "apple of gold" to us. The Union and the Constitution are the picture of silver, subsequently framed around it. The picture was made for the apple—not the apple for the picture. Let us act that neither the picture or apple are ever blurred, bruised or broken. The doctrine of self-government is right—absolutely and eternally right. It is the sheet-anchor of American republicanism.[8]

No one has done as much as Abraham Lincoln to explain what America commits to be and become.

But Lincoln's words also admit, at least obliquely, the gaping chasm between what we profess and what we secure—the purportedly "partial and temporary departures from necessity." There was his attested commitment that "in due time the weights will be lifted from the shoulders of all." In "due" time—partial, temporary, execrable, enduring, and marginalizing "departures," which would prove crushing to the "declared" and "dedicated" foundational principle.

The most generous view of American history, no doubt, is that of the too slow, tragic, often-bloodied, and too modest but still determined expansion of the reach and membership of the governing notion of "equality" and "liberty to all" as it "entwines itself [more] closely about the human heart."

This unfolding progress is reflected partially in the text of the Constitution itself. The Thirteenth, Fourteenth, Fifteenth, Nineteenth, Twenty-Fourth, and Twenty-Sixth Amendments reflect its expansion. And in broader movements of constitutional and statutory equality, the "constantly spreading and deepening influence" of the foundational charge appears.

Breaking the Promise That Binds

But this grudging progress is only part of the American story. Throughout our history, as Heather Cox Richardson has argued, the United States has "swung between the defense of equality outlined in the Declaration of Independence ... our peculiar history of racism" and "the defense of private property," which is said to be rooted in our traditions. "Every time it seems we are approaching equality before the law," she writes, "those determined to prevent that equality" rise to "turn people against it." In this recurring argument, the idea that "an equal say in our government for all people amounts to socialism," atheism, or worse always arises.[9]

North Carolina's history is peppered with such backlash. Battles over equality, particularly concerning the electoral franchise, have played out through emancipatory struggles and conservative retrenchments. Efforts to suppress participation have been endlessly creative. Sometimes, they have been explicitly racial and hideously violent. Other restrictions have been couched in more euphemistic terms: "corruption," "fraud," "law and order," "good government," "ballot integrity," "accountability," "local control," "state's rights," and the like. As Robert Korstad and James Leloudis have shown, "throughout all these [struggles], the core issues have remained the same, equality and the right of all citizens to participate fully in a democratic society." Understood in historical context, they claim, today's conflicts over voting and civil rights in North Carolina remind us that we live in similarly consequential times. Then, as now, "democracy is imperiled by divisive racial appeals, violent expressions of white supremacy, and efforts to roll back newly won rights." Our history thus provides "a clarifying power."[10] The pushback, it seems, always comes.

The pages of this book echo the same unworthy and tragic pattern. Shocking numbers of Tar Heels apparently could not abide Barack Obama's election in 2008. Republicans took over both houses of the General Assembly two years later. All-white Republican caucuses ruled the roost. They quickly drew state and federal election districts to intentionally discriminate against Black residents. They manipulated the electoral system, with "surgical precision," to handicap African Americans. They repealed statutes that afforded relief for racial discrimination in both the civil and criminal justice systems. They attempted to effectively overturn municipal elections in which Black candidates prevailed. They passed programs designed to increase racial segregation in the public schools. They reacted to Black Lives Matter protests by making it harder to obtain police video footage. They moved to permanently protect Confederate monuments. They even worked to prohibit the teaching of our actual racial history to kids. The theory seems to be, why trouble children with such matters? We're not troubled. This is the fairest society in history. Just be sure to limit your gaze.

The list of outrages is long, and lawmakers prefer, again, that it not be emphasized. They do all this while recognizing that 40 percent of Tar Heels are persons of color and that the state will be majority minority in a few short decades. So the clock is ticking.[11] If they have to choose between white ascendancy and the Declaration of Independence's commitment to the equal rights of humankind, then apparently, it's an easy choice. Power, not democracy, is what matters. Save your equality talk for the Fourth of July.

Evangelical voters and their lawmakers, the stoutest Republicans, joined their colleagues in cheating to distort electoral districts. They adopted new polling rules to handicap Black people, whom they apparently regard as their adversaries. They've talked much of religious accommodation, but they have actually used their new government powers to force their secular opponents to pay for religious schools. Though they are a decided minority of North Carolinians, they moved to enforce their religious views about abortion on everybody else. They did the same to try to stop gay folks from marrying the ones they love and to humiliate transgender Tar Heels in bathrooms and locker rooms. They insisted that everyone should embrace their prayers at governmental and public educational functions. And, most pointedly, they continually claimed that anti-discrimination laws can't be applied to them because they deserve special immunities. If North Carolina must decide between equality for all and white, Christian ascendancy, then they're old school, suggesting, "We count; you don't"—as ever.

Republican legislators control the state, but they fear the numbers are increasingly mounting against them. So, they have acted to avoid the perils of one person–one vote. They became the world's experts (or, at least, they hire the world's experts) in redistricting fraud. They tampered with the voting process in any way they could devise to hurt their adversaries. They messed with judicial elections. They debilitated the other branches of government if their favorite candidates weren't selected. There is to be no separation of powers in their regime. All previously "public" institutions in this state—such as schools and universities—now exist principally for their plunder. All power is theirs, especially the power to entrench their power, and old-fashioned notions like independent judicial review and municipal prerogative have been deemed exactly that—old fashioned.

They are not, to be sure, the party of Lincoln. If Lincoln placed democracy over partisan power, then in their view, he was a fool. They won't follow him down that naive path. They're out to ensure government of the Republicans, by the Republicans, and for the Republicans. No more need be said. If the rest believe in democracy, too bad. They didn't win in 2010, when Republicans apparently obtained the eternal power to slant the North Carolina "democracy" in their direction. Besides, North Carolina Republicans are not as bad as George Wallace or Lester Maddox. So everyone else should shut up and take their medicine.

Each of these powerful North Carolina cadres has this in common: they have determined that their commitment to democracy prevails only if they win. If they can't muster a majority, then they demand to govern nonetheless. Our pledges of allegiance, the Declaration of Independence, the Gettysburg Address, and constitutional guarantees of equal protection under the laws are to simply to be set aside if they get in the way of these preferred folks' continued power. The only self-evident truth, for them, is their inherent right to dominate.

A North Carolina Sedition Caucus

These equality-denying measures occurred at the hands of the North Carolina General Assembly. But any quick tour through the Tar Heel

State's steps to crush the foundations of self-government must make at least brief mention of our apparently (more) formal, federal North Carolina sedition caucus. Mark Meadows, a former N.C. representative, was former president Trump's chief of staff. In that role, he repeatedly, directly, and surely illegally aided and abetted Trump's efforts to overthrow the 2020 election.[12] Madison Cawthorn, another of our N.C. Republican representatives, pumped up the crowd that sought to overthrow the government by violent insurrection in Washington, D.C., on January 6, 2021. Cawthorn's western North Carolina colleague Rep. Virginia Foxx was giddy to make the successful motion to expel Liz Cheney from House Republican leadership because she refused to embrace Trump's obvious lies about the 2020 presidential race. Foxx taunted Cheney as "a leader who has no followers"—almost bragging about the absence of character in the Republican House caucus.[13]

The *New York Times* reported that Republican former N.C. Supreme Court Chief Justice Mark Martin offered his studied advice to the former president that former vice president Mike Pence had the right to reject the election's certification. Sidney Powell, a Republican North Carolina lawyer, presented stunning conspiracy theories—in court and out—on behalf of Trump and his campaign, though she later asserted that any sensible person would have known she was lying. In December 2020, all but two Republicans who represented North Carolina in the U.S. House of Representatives signed on to an absurd Texas lawsuit falsely claiming that the presidential election was "tainted with fraud" and should be overturned. Republican representative Dan Bishop distributed an eight-page "report" blaming Democrats for a national effort to "weaken ballot security and provide opportunities for ballot-box stuffing." He then joined two-thirds of the North Carolina Republican congressional delegation in voting, even after the murderous coup attempt unfolded, to award the 2020 presidential contest to the losing candidate. Bishop, Cawthorn, and Foxx, along with Reps. Richard Hudson, Greg Murphy, and David Rouzer and former representative Ted Budd, cast ballots to illegally throw out the election results. In November 2022, Budd was elected to an open U.S. Senate seat.[14]

When Sen. Richard Burr voted to hold former president Trump accountable for instigating a violent rebellion, the North Carolina Republican Party called an "emergency" meeting to unanimously censure Burr for his heresy.[15] In short, a formal, attested autocratic movement is alive and well in North Carolina. And it is powerfully positioned. The North Carolina pushback against "the equal political rights of mankind" is potent—and growing.

A Wounded Constitutionalism

To understate, there is much to regret in this now decade-long battle against democracy in the Tar Heel State and beyond. First, as I have argued, constitutional lawyers on both the right and left have long assumed a set of givens in the United States. There will and should be ample, continuing, and enthusiastic policy disagreement in this constitutional democracy. We argue relentlessly about the budget, taxes, spending levels, economic rights, subsidies, infrastructure, environmental issues, climate change, regulatory burdens, teacher salaries, labor issues, commercial development, and more. The list is literally endless—and evolving. On all these fronts, we propose, debate, lobby, form coalitions, hustle, and embrace the tools of politics, recognizing that in the end, the majority's preferences will prevail.

But constitutionalists also necessarily assume that on an array of other fronts, we agree. These are the foundations of constitutional democracy, its shared understandings.[16] They are, in essence, the rules of the road that allow democracy to actually function. Often, they are clear, robust, even textual mandates like the right to vote; the right to speak; freedom of the press; the right to assemble, protest, and organize; the right to free and unhindered elections; the right to fair representation; the right to equal participation; and the like. It takes no great perceptiveness to see that, on some level, such rules must be developed and enforced if the democratic venture is to endure. It's not unlike the rules in a town hall meeting giving everyone an equal shot at the microphone—lest the undertaking no longer actually be a meeting of the town.

And often, these foundational rules are softer, more fluid, and more malleable. Rules like the separation of powers, checks and balances, federalism, local government prerogative, academic independence and governance, and deference to organizations of civil society and religious belief are also methods of ensuring that a robust and balanced democratic society has the breathing room to function without authorities becoming dangerously amassed in too-narrow confines. Sensible governments don't allow too much power to be concentrated in too few hands. And though we might not be as readily able to precisely identify the lines of demarcation, we understand and embrace the need for diffusion—for no other reason than our own safety.

These guardrail norms, hard and soft, are the givens, the shared commitments of constitutional democracy, in North Carolina and in the United States overall. And our general framework, we've thought, is that we all agree on these pathways as we fight about most everything else. In fact, it's that agreement that allows us to effectively and accountably fight on all the other fronts. When you lose the election to control the statehouse, you don't burn down the Legislative Building on your last day in office. You go home, gather yourself, regroup, organize, learn from your mistakes, and try again next time.

Over the last decade in North Carolina, we've learned that the shared commitment to these foundational standards is decidedly weaker than constitutional stalwarts might have assumed. The mistake was perhaps an understandable one because these are, broadly speaking, the norms that we pledge allegiance to, fight our wars for, sing our hymns about, recite hopefully to our children, and attest to as providing the mission and meaning of our nation. In fact, they've turned out to be weaker, less durable, more contested, and far more willingly discarded than I and many others had presumed.

If one was inclined to be generous, it could be said that sometimes these breaches may have come from what could be labeled as inexperience or overexuberance arising from the assumption of newly acquired powers. I think a lot of the General Assembly's moves to run roughshod over institutions like the academy or even the judiciary in this way. The most frequent refrain I heard in my run-ins with Republican lawmakers and trustees was that I had better get it through my head that there's a new sheriff in town, and if I knew what was good for me, I'd better join the posse—that the folks who sign your paychecks will tell you what to say and when to say it. Such is the way of the world, the theory goes, even if an actual university or (more importantly) an impartial court of law couldn't possibly operate in such a fashion.

But much of the North Carolina crusade against democracy comes from highly informed and experienced sources. N.C. Senate President Pro Tempore Phil Berger and N.C. Speaker of the House Tim Moore are knowledgeable, senior lawyers. They are the principal architects of the overarching assault. Their staffing henchmen are effective and expert. The Republican redistricting and voting-regulation leaders of both chambers have been, over the decades, among the world's leading manipulators of the political process. They knew precisely the impact that the denials of equality that they strove to inflict would have; that's explicitly what they were after. In addition, these folks are heavy participants in national Republican networks that are out to thwart majority rule. When these leaders, seasoned and otherwise, have been joined to a much broader political base that has obviously come to accept and even cheer for the destruction of traditional constitutional guardrails, the underlying preconditions of democratic government have been dramatically damaged. That's tough news for any constitutional lawyer—or any citizen. It also forcefully reminds us of the strength of the ancient and ever-present lust for power.

Second, as is all too apparent, Democratic Party opposition to an all-out battle for democracy is incapable of embracing the urgency, the resolve, the will, and the steel-driven strength to meet the literally existential challenges of the day. Perhaps it's because Democrats have engaged in politics in a defensive posture for so long, fretting to show that above all else they aren't as bad as the Republicans, that they've lost the talent for leadership and meaning. After all, a watered-down Republican agenda is still a Republican agenda, and the claim that one is a weaker, paler version of one's adversary hardly spurs others to take the hill. But most Democratic standard-bearers, here and across the country, fail to behave as if they understand that the American experiment actually hangs in the balance.

It's almost as if they aren't paying attention. So, they do what they've always done: demand a little more money for this or that program or profess their un-acted-upon fealty to climate change or gun control as anti-democratic forces prepare steadily for battle. Or perhaps Democrats assume that someone else will step in and save them—here in North Carolina, perhaps it will be the Moral Monday movement, the Southern Coalition for Social Justice, the American Civil Liberties Union (ACLU), Common Cause, or Black Lives Matter. Regardless of the fantasy, they aren't obliged to actually *do* anything. They're Democrats—they talk; they don't act. Things will work out, all facts to the contrary.

Third, and finally, it's now clear that the courts won't save us, though that lesson comes more resoundingly from Washington, D.C., than from Raleigh. A half century of mostly Republican Supreme Court appointments has promised, disingenuously, justices who would play honest referee, honor precedent, and be guided closely by the text and history of the Constitution. Instead, the most activist, partisan, and deeply ideological court in American history has been launched. Its legacy will be aimed at privileging wealth, right-wing Christianity, and white ascendancy over democracy and equality. The unknown, at this point, is how much damage to the American experiment they'll be allowed to inflict before the institution is effectively dismantled. In the past decade, North Carolina has benefitted notably from the remnant protections of independent federal judicial review. But, in the final analysis, all federal judges will be required to bend the knee to the United States Supreme Court, and that means they'll have no future constructive role in the cause of justice.

Engaged, Dedicated, Morally Outraged Citizens

There are but two parties now, traitors and patriots.
—Ulysses Grant, 1861

As Donald Trump bullies the Republican Party nationally and Republican-dominated legislatures across the country move to further limit their adversaries' electoral rights, I'm not certain that most North Carolinians recognize their democracy is seriously imperiled. Most are reluctant to conclude that an array of their leaders is out to end the American political experiment. But, as in nineteenth-century North Carolina, we now have a massive group among us willing to throw over democracy in order to ensure their ascendancy.

With a dominant political party committed to autocracy, we're treading new ground—at least new ground for modern times. Many of our leaders, here and across the country, have proven themselves unfit to govern, unfit to be trusted with moral and political leadership. That won't change. They've shown their surprising stripes. There is no unity to be had or sought with people who don't believe in the American promise. There is no compromise to be had with authoritarianism. Meeting seditionists halfway only makes one complicit in a war against democracy. The pro-democratic forces in this defining struggle can't be the gentle ones, the sweet and civil opposition. The stakes are too high. As an unfolding diverse, pluralistic society presents itself, Republicans—nationally and in the Tar Heel State—seek to thwart its development, ditching traditional bromides of equality and self-government in favor of the permanent dominance of the white, the Christian, the straight, and the moneyed. Our founding and defining commitments are literally put into play. As Heather Cox Richardson has written, "This is not the only story from today, but it is the only story that historians will note from this era—did Americans defend their democracy?"[17]

Frederick Douglass offered eloquent and inspiring direction for such times, referring, unsurprisingly, to the launching Declaration of Independence:

I would call to mind the sublime and glorious truths with which, at its birth, it saluted a listening world. Its voice then, was as the trump of an archangel, summoning hoary forms of oppression and time honored tyranny to judgment. It announced the advent of a nation, based upon human brotherhood and the self-evident truths of liberty and equality. Its mission was the redemption of the world from the bondage of ages. Apply these sublime and glorious truths to the situation now before you. Put away your race prejudice. Banish the idea that one class must rule over another. Recognize the fact that the rights of the humblest citizen are as worthy of protection as are those of the highest, and your problem will be solved; whether it shall have foes without, or foes within, based upon the eternal principles of truth, justice and humanity, your Republic will stand and flourish forever.[18]

Nor was Douglass unclear about the necessary tone:

It is not light that is needed, but fire; it is not the gentle shower, but thunder. We need the storm, the whirlwind, and the earthquake. The feeling of the nation must be quickened; the conscience of the nation must be roused; the propriety of the nation must be startled; the hypocrisy of the nation must be exposed.[19]

The South has always been a pivotal place in American struggles for equality. As my friend from the Moral Monday efforts, Roz Pelles, has put it, the South is "where change needs to happen most and it has also been a place that has catalyzed change, the two are connected."[20] Reverend Barber has echoed the claim: "If you are going to change the nation, you have to change the South, and if you're going to change the South, you have to focus on these legislatures."[21]

I've offered less-than-embracing views of the courts and of the traditional Democratic Party in these pages. I should probably be clearer. I don't argue for a third political party. The exigency is too great. The time is too short. The Democratic Party is the only game in town. Maybe it is more precise to say that, in my old age, I've come to have less faith in law

and in partisan Democratic politics but more faith in the power of engaged, dedicated, morally outraged citizens to do the work of saving democracy. If we are, in Lincoln's words, to rededicate ourselves "to the fundamental maxims of a free society," then it'll come from these folks, not
consultants and pollsters and the timid cobblers and patchers who often
dominate our partisan politics. Change must come through the Democratic Party, but it likely won't come from the Democratic Party.

Maybe it's not inaccurate to say, by way of illustration, that the election
of President Biden itself was an example of such efforts. At the bottom,
it was a committed, courageous, and immensely diverse citizenry that
confronted the budding dictatorship of the vilest president in American
history and cast him out. The victory was made all the more astounding
in that it was attributable to no compelling or charismatic leader—just
great hearts from every walk of life across an extraordinarily broad nation.
Biden's election produced the highest vote totals seen in decades. They
were secured by brave, unbowed, often elderly poll workers saying to the
bullies and blowhards, "Step aside; we've got this." Young folks marched
and registered. Previously disengaged citizens poured out of the streets
and into the polling booths. They said with pride and power that they
were unwilling to surrender the meaning of their nation. No political class
saved America. Believers did.

In my view, the same could be said of the breathtaking rejection of an
abortion ban by Kansas voters in August 2022. Kansas was the first state to
vote on abortion after the norm-shattering *Dobbs* decision by the United
States Supreme Court. Political observers, particularly professional ones,
sleepily assumed that Kansas would follow traditional Republican, purportedly pro-life, patterns—not so, decidedly not so.

Instead, Kansas voters supported abortion rights by sweeping margins. Rachel Sweet, the head of Kansas for Constitutional Freedom, the
main pro-choice group opposing the amendment, said, "The people of
Kansas have spoken. The victory was huge and decisive." They think that
"abortion should be safe, legal and accessible in the state of Kansas," she
explained. They flatly demanded it. Jae Mayer, a twenty-three-year-old

who was stirred to activism by the battle, said, "It's never looked like this in Kansas before. I'm so proud of my state right now." Emily Wales, the president and CEO of Planned Parenthood Great Plains Votes, rightly boasted, "Anti-abortion politicians put this amendment on the primary ballot with the goal of a low turnout, but they discounted Kansans, who said loud and clear they believe and trust patients to make their own medical decisions."[22]

Republicans were stunned by the results, of course. But none were more surprised than traditional Democratic politicians and consultants. Who knew that citizens could be stirred by conscience? Who knew that regular folks would straighten their backs and fight? Apparently, the people of Kansas did. Democracy ain't dead yet. It's not all up to the politicians.

These last years have been unnerving. We've been somewhat undone. People like Trump and his North Carolina consigliere Mark Meadows have exuded a venom that threatens to engulf us all. They almost convince us, by accretion, that there's no honor in being human. There's no character, no morality, no courage, no obligation, no duty, no integrity, no idealism, no meaning, no love, and no habit of heart. There is only the more powerful crushing the less advantaged, only the villain stalking his prey.

But even as an old man, I'm confident that these loathsome types cannot prevail. It is singular and crucial work that we are in. Deeply diverse societies often founder, brutalizing the most vulnerable in ways that demolish the humanity of all.[23] And no decent person can abide this fate. So this is tough work—the toughest. Now, the United States' and North Carolina's defining attestations are put inescapably to the test. Many, apparently, would bolt from the historic commitment, insisting on privilege rather than long-declared principle—but not all of us, not even most of us. And the mission, it turns out, is of the highest order. We learn slowly, grudgingly, but finally, here, that we can't be only the heirs of freedom; we must also be its guarantors. We can't claim only liberty's gift without also assuming its obligation. We've come to understand, even if reluctantly, that democracy is never a final achievement; it is a call to an unending struggle.[24] We believe that the arc of the moral universe does indeed bend toward justice, but we understand that that's the case only if we ourselves do the bending.[25] Most crucially, we utterly refuse to give up on the notion of an America for all, even when it hangs frighteningly in the balance—especially when it hangs frighteningly in the balance.

Introduction

1. Michael Fletcher, "An Unimpeded GOP Veers North Carolina to the Right," *Washington Post* (May 20, 2013); Editorial, "The Decline of North Carolina," *New York Times* (July 9, 2013); Jason Zengerle, "Is North Carolina the Future of American Politics?" *New York Times Magazine* (June 20, 2017), quoting Rob Christensen; Karen Cox, "What's the Matter with North Carolina?" *New York Times* (December 19, 2016); Rob Schofield, "Altered State: How 5 Years of Conservative Rule Have Redefined North Carolina," *NC Policy Watch* (December 1, 2015).

2. Fletcher, *supra* note 1; Editorial, *supra* note 1; Zengerle, *supra* note 1 (quoting Rob Christensen).

3. Editorial, *supra* note 1.

4. Ibid.

5. Ibid.

6. Cox, *supra* note 1.

7. Ibid.

8. "Joint Resolution Condemning the University of North Carolina Board of Governors and System Office," American Association of University Professors (June 2022), https://www.aaup.org/sites/default/files/Joint-Resolution-Condemning-the-North-Carolina-Board-of-Governors-and-System-Office.pdf; Jane Stancill, "National Group Joins Chorus Opposed to Closing UNC's Poverty Center," *Raleigh News & Observer* (February 14, 2015).

9. Kate Murphy, "National Group Condemns UNC," *Raleigh News & Observer* (June 22, 2022), https://www.newsobserver.com/news/local/education/article 262597172.html; "Joint Resolution Condemning the University of North Carolina Board of Governors and System Office," *supra* note 8. The AAUP concluded, "The documentation of instances of broken governance, severe violations of academic freedom, and patterns of institutional racism caused by long-standing political interference and cowardly top-down administration speaks volumes about the severity of the underlying problems at UNC."

10. Gene Nichol, *Indecent Assembly: The North Carolina Legislature's Blueprint for the War on Democracy and Equality* (Blair, 2019).

11. Steven F. Hayward, "Ronald Reagan's Shiny City of Exceptional Immigrants," *Forbes* (December 6, 2013), https://www.forbes.com/sites/stevenhayward

/2013/12/06/ronald-reagans-shining-city-of-exceptional-immigrants/?sh=5a99aa41639f.

12. See Gene Nichol, "Children of Distant Fathers: Sketching an Ethos of Constitutional Liberty," *Wisconsin Law Review* 1319 (1985).

13. Lyndon Johnson, "Speech Introducing the Voting Rights Act," Washington, D.C. (March 15, 1965), https://www.archives.gov/legislative/features/voting-rights-1965/johnson.html. See also Gene Nichol, "Betraying Decency and Democracy in North Carolina," *Facing South* (June 10, 2021), https://www.facingsouth.org/2021/06/voices-betraying-decency-and-democracy-north-carolina.

14. Nichol, *supra* note 13.

15. Roger Cohen has put the national issue (with Donald Trump) this way: "White Christian males losing their place in the social order decided they'd do anything to save themselves, and to heck with morality. They made a bargain with the devil in full knowledge. So the real question is: What does it mean to be an American today? Who are we, goddamit?"

16. Roger Davis, *The Wilmington Coup of 1898: How America's Most Infamous Race Riot Led to the Growth of White Supremacy* (self-published, 2021). Roger Cohen, "How Far Has America Fallen?" *New York Times* (August 24, 2018), https://www.nytimes.com/2018/08/24/opinion/trump-colorado-purple-state.html.

17. See James L. Leloudis and Robert R. Korstad, *Fragile Democracy: The Struggle over Race and Voting Rights in North Carolina* (University of North Carolina Press, 2020), 3.

18. Frederick Douglass, "The Lessons of the Hour," Washington, D.C. (January 9, 1894).

Chapter 1

1. Emmanuel Felton and Cleve R. Wootson Jr., "Black Activists Say the Time for Pretty Speeches Is Over. They Need an Action Plan from Biden on Voting Rights," *Washington Post* (January 11, 2022).

2. Gene Nichol, "In NC, All Diversity Sits on One Side of the Aisle," *Raleigh News & Observer* (January 20, 2019), https://www.newsobserver.com/opinion/article224507140.html.

3. See Carl Smith, "Blacks in State Legislatures: A State-by-State Map," *Governing Magazine* (January 13, 2021), https://www.governing.com/now/blacks-in-state-legislatures-a-state-by-state-map.html.

4. Pew Research Center, "Racial, Ethnic Diversity Increases Yet Again with the

117th Congress," https://www.pewresearch.org/fact-tank/2021/01/28/racial-ethnic-diversity-increases-yet-again-with-the-117th-congress/ (January 28, 2021). In 2020, former representative Mia Love was the only Black Republican woman in the U.S. House of Representatives. In 2021, there were none.

5. The seepings of the heart do, sadly, slip out into the public domain on occasion. See, for example, Robert Pittenger's statements to the BBC during the Charlotte demonstrations in response to the police killing of Keith Lamont Scott. The former representative for North Carolina's Ninth District (and former N.C. General Assembly member) explained to the BBC that the Black demonstrators on the streets of Charlotte "hate white people because white people are successful and they're not." Peter Holley, "Congressman: Charlotte Protestors 'Hate White People Because White People Are Successful,'" *Washington Post* (September 23, 2016), https://www.washingtonpost.com/news/post-nation/wp/2016/09/22/charlotte-protesters-hate-white-people-because-white-people-are-successful-congressman-claims/?utm_term=.bcbfe6c7970a.

6. Gene Nichol, "Suppressing the Black Vote," *Winston-Salem Journal* (September 22, 2016), https://journalnow.com/opinion/columnists/gene-nichol-suppressing-the-black-vote/article_11af9bd2-1959-5427-a8ab-0f1e34dcf278.html.

7. Covington v. North Carolina, 316 F.R.D. 117, 124 (M.D.N.C. 2016).

8. Covington v. North Carolina, 270 F. Supp. 3d at 844, 897, 902 (2017).

9. Covington, *supra* note 7; Covington, *supra* note 8.

10. NAACP v. McCrory, U.S. Court of Appeals for the Fourth Circuit, July 29, 2016, no. 16-1468.

11. See Ari Berman, "North Carolina Passes the Country's Worst Voter Suppression Law," *The Nation* (July 26, 2013).

12. Anne Blythe, "Federal Judge Invalidates Greensboro Redistricting Plan," *Raleigh News & Observer* (April 3, 2017).

13. Ibid.

14. See Gene Nichol, *Indecent Assembly: The North Carolina Legislature's Blueprint for the War on Democracy and Equality* (Blair, 2019), 21–24.

15. Michael Gordon, Mark Price, and Katie Peralta, "Understanding HB2: North Carolina's New State Law Solidifies State Role in Defining Discrimination," *Charlotte Observer* (March 26, 2016), https://www.charlotteobserver.com>article 68401147. See also "Understanding HB2," *The State* (March 26, 2016); Brady Dennis, "'Wrong Beyond Repair.' 'The Worst in Us.' N.C. Papers Blast Transgender Bathroom Law," *Washington Post* (March 25, 2016).

16. See Nichol, *supra* note 14 at 22–26.

17. See ibid. at 23–26.

18. See WTVD, "Cooper Vetoes Bill Opposing Critical Race Theory in Schools," *ABC11* (September 10, 2021), https://abc11.com/critical-race-theory-crt -in-schools-what-is/11012907/. See also Nyamekye Daniel, "Critical Race Theory Bill Heads to North Carolina Governor," *The Center Square* (September 1, 2021), https://www.thecentersquare.com/north_carolina/critical-race-theory-bill-heads -to-north-carolina-governor/article_9b8bf922-0b4b-11ec-b6c4-db130db6ffd1 .html.

19. Rob Schofield, "Gene Nichol: The Absurd Practical Effect of Johnston County's School Curriculum Censorship Policy," *NC Policy Watch* (October 27, 2021), https://pulse.ncpolicywatch.org/2021/10/27/gene-nichol-the-absurd-practical -effect-of-johnston-countys-school-curriculum-censorship-policy/#sthash.IqXptVIP .dpbs.

20. Laura Meckler and Hannah Natanson, "New Critical Race Theory Laws Have Teachers Scared, Confused and Self-Censoring," *Washington Post* (February 14, 2022), https://www.washingtonpost.com/education/2022/02/14/critical -race-theory-teachers-fear-laws/.

21. Rob Schofield, "NC GOP's Judicial Impeachment Threats Are a New Low in Trump-Like Lawlessness," *NC Policy Watch* (January 25, 2022), https://ncpolicy watch.com/2022/01/25/nc-gops-judicial-impeachment-threats-are-a-new-low-in -trump-like-lawlessness/.

22. Jason Zengerle, "Is North Carolina the Future of American Politics?" *New York Times* (June 20, 2017).

23. See Gene Nichol, "Lessons on Political Speech, Academic Freedom, and University Governance from the New North Carolina," *First Amendment Law Review* 16 (Fall 2017), http://www.ncpolicywatch.com/wp-content/uploads/2018/02 /Nichol-First-Amendment-Law-Review-article.pdf.

24. Jeffrey J. Crow, Paul D. Escott, and Flora J. Hatley Wadelington, *A History of African Americans in North Carolina* (University of North Carolina Press, 1992).

25. James L. Leloudis and Robert R. Korstad, *Fragile Democracy: The Struggle over Race and Voting Rights in North Carolina* (University of North Carolina Press, 2020), 3.

26. Ibid. at 4.

27. Eric Foner, *The Second Founding: How the Civil War and Reconstruction Remade the Constitution* (W. W. Norton, 2019).

28. Ronald Brownstein, "Why Republican Voter Restrictions Are a Race Against Time," *CNN* (March 23, 2021), https://www.cnn.com/2021/03/23/politics/voting -rights-republicans-bills-demographics/index.html.

29. Ibid.

30. Ibid.

31. Leloudis and Korstad, *supra* note 25 at 124.

32. Ibid. at 124.

33. U.S. Const. amend. XIV.

34. James E. Bond, "Ratification of the Fourteenth Amendment in North Carolina," *Wake Forest Law Review* 20 (1984): 89, https://digitalcommons.law.seattleu.edu/cgi/viewcontent.cgi?referer=&httpsredir=1&article=1325&context=faculty.

35. Ibid.

36. Ibid.

37. Ibid.

38. Ibid.

39. Richard L. Aynes, "The Continuing Importance of Congressman John Bingham and the Fourteenth Amendment," *Akron Law Review* 36, no. 4 (2003): 615, https://ideaexchange.uakron.edu/akronlawreview/vol36/iss4/1/.

40. Ibid.

41. Rick Hasen, "Divided Three Judge Court Holds North Carolina Congressional Redistricting an Unconstitutional Partisan Gerrymander, Considers New Districts for 2018 Elections," *Election Law Blog* (August 27, 2018); Gene Nichol, "NC Has the Worst Gerrymander in US History. What Else Is New?" *Raleigh News & Observer* (February 1, 2018).

42. Common Cause v. Rucho, 318 F. Supp. 777 (M.D.N.C. 2018).

43. Ibid.

44. Nichol, *supra* note 14 at 16–30.

45. Mark Joseph Stern, "North Carolina Republicans' Legislative Coup Is an Attack on Democracy," *Slate* (December 15, 2016); John Nichols, "State Republicans Are Refusing to Honor the Peaceful Transition of Power," *The Nation* (December 4, 2018).

46. Nichol, *supra* note 14 at ch. 4.

47. Ibid. at ch. 5.

48. See ibid. at 64–67.

49. Ibid. at 108–125.

50. Ibid. at 144–56.

51. Bruce Springsteen, "Long Walk Home," track 10 on *Magic*, Columbia Records (2007).

52. See Robert D. McFadden, "Rosanell Eaton, Fierce Voting Rights Advocate, Dies at 97," *New York Times* (December 9, 2018).

53. See the *Nation*, "Exclusive: Zach Galifinakis Wants You to Know How Bad Gerrymandering Has Gotten," YouTube (September 20, 2016), https://america dividedseries.com/democracy-for-sale/.

54. McFadden, *supra* note 52.

55. Ibid.

56. Ibid.

57. Leslie Ovalle, "Remembering Rosanell Eaton, an Outspoken Advocate for Voting Rights," *NPR* (December 12, 2018).

58. Ibid.

59. McFadden, *supra* note 52.

60. Ibid.

61. Ibid.

62. Noam Chomsky, *Requiem for the American Dream: The 10 Principles of Concentration of Wealth and Power* (Seven Stories Press, 2017), quoting Howard Zinn.

Chapter 2

1. Obergefell v. Hodges, 135 S. Ct. 2071 (2015).

2. Mark Binker, "Graham Ad Backs Marriage Amendment," *WRAL* (May 2, 2012), https://www.wral.com/news/state/nccapitol/blogpost/11054540/.

3. Cacky Catlett, "Rev. Franklin Graham Voices Support of Amendment One," *WWAY 3* (April 28, 2012), https://www.wwaytv3.com/rev-franklin-graham-voices -support-of-amendment-one/.

4. Rachel Weiner, "North Carolina Passes Gay Marriage Ban Amendment One," *Washington Post* (May 8, 2012), https://www.washingtonpost.com/blogs/the -fix/post/north-carolina-passes-gay-marriage-ban-amendment-one/2012/05/08 /gIQAHYpfBU_blog.html.

5. "Talking Points: Notable Quotes from a Week of News," *Dallas Morning News* (May 12, 2012), https://www.dallasnews.com/opinion/commentary/2012/05/12 /talking-points-notable-quotes-from-a-week-of-news/.

6. Obergefell v. Hodges, 135 S. Ct. 2071 (2015).

7. Mark Berman, "North Carolina Bill Banning Same-Sex Marriage Again Won't Be Heard, House Speaker Says," *Washington Post* (April 12, 2017).

8. Joe Killian, "Bill Filed to Defy Supreme Court Ruling, Oppose Same-Sex Marriage in N.C.," *NC Policy Watch* (February 14, 2019), https://pulse.ncpolicy watch.org/2019/02/14/bill-filed-to-defy-supreme-court-ruling-oppose-same-sex -marriage-in-n-c/#sthash.JBsVHU4y.dpbs.

9. Ibid; Mark Joseph Stern, "North Carolina Passes Law Allowing Magistrates

to Refuse to Marry Same-Sex Couples," *Slate* (June 11, 2015), https://slate.com /human-interest/2015/06/north-carolina-passes-law-letting-magistrates-claim -religious-exemption.html.

10. Stern, *supra* note 9.

11. Colin Campbell, "NC House Votes 65–45 to Exempt Magistrates from Marriage Duties," *Raleigh News & Observer* (May 27, 2015), https://www.newsobserver .com/news/politics-government/article22433973.html. See Emma Green, "Why North Carolina Judges Can Still Refuse to Perform Same-Sex Marriages," *The Atlantic* (September 21, 2016), https://www.theatlantic.com/politics/archive/2016/09 /north-carolina-magistrates-judges-same-sex-marriage-dismissals/500996/; Anne Blythe, "Should NC Magistrates Be Able to Opt Out of Performing Marriages on Religious Grounds? Case at 4th Circuit," *Raleigh News & Observer* (May 10, 2017), https://www.newsobserver.com/news/politics-government/state-politics/article 149569774.html; Gene Nichol, "Drawing the Line between Law and Religious Freedom," *Raleigh News & Observer* (June 10, 2017), https://www.newsobserver .com/opinion /op-ed/article155510484.html.

12. Dave Philipps, "North Carolina Bans Local Anti-Discrimination Policies," *New York Times* (March 23, 2016).

13. Michael Gordon, Mark S. Price, and Katie Peralta, "Understanding HB2: North Carolina's New Law Solidifies State Role in Defining Discrimination," *Charlotte Observer* (March 26, 2016), http://www.charlotteobserver.com/news/politics -government/article68401147.html#storylink=cpy (quoting Maxine Eichner). See also "Understanding HB2," *The State* (March 26, 2016), https://www.thestate.com /news/politics-government/article68401147.html.

14. Philipps, *supra* note 12.

15. See, generally, Brady Dennis, "'Wrong Beyond Repair.' 'The Worst in U.S.' N.C. Papers Blast Transgender Bathroom Law," *Washington Post* (March 25, 2016), https://www.washingtonpost.com/news/post-nation/wp/2016/03/25/wrong -beyond-repair-the-worst-in-us-n-c-papers-blast-transgender-bathroom-law/?utm _term =.13b34bd055ab.

16. See Maureen O'Hare, "U.K. Issues Travel Warning about Anti-LGBT Laws in U.S. States," *CNN* (April 22, 2016), https://www.cnn.com/travel/article/uk -lgbt-travel -advice-north-carolina-mississippi/index.html.

17. "'Bathroom Bill' to Cost North Carolina $3.76 Billion," *CNBC* (March 27, 2017); Christy Mallory and Brad Sears, "The Legal and Economic Implications of North Carolina's HB2," *Williams Institute* (May 11, 2016), https://williamsinstitute .law.ucla.edu/publications/legal-economic-implications-hb2/.

18. See, generally, Gene Nichol, *Indecent Assembly: The North Carolina Legis-*

lature's Blueprint for the War on Democracy and Equality (Blair, 2019), ch. 5. See also Amber Phillips, "The Tumultuous History of North Carolina's Bathroom Bill, Which Is on Its Way to Repeal," *Washington Post* (March 30, 2017), https://www.washingtonpost.com/news/the-fix/wp/2016/12/19/the-tumultuous-recent-history-of-north-carolinas-bathroom-bill-which-could-be-repealed/; David A. Graham, "North Carolina Overturns LGBT-Discrimination Bans," *The Atlantic* (March 24, 2016), https://www.theatlantic.com/politics/archive/2016/03/north-carolina-lgbt-discrimination-transgender-bathrooms/475125.

19. Rob Schofield, "Why Did Religious Right Support a Bill to Enable Discrimination against Christians?" *NC Policy Watch* (March 30, 2016).

20. "Email documents obtained by the *Charlotte Business Journal* (CBJ), reveal that Rep. Dan Bishop, the lead author of North Carolina's deeply discriminatory HB2 law, compared LGBTQ people and supporters of equality to the 'Taliban' and made numerous other disparaging comments. According to the documents, a supporter of Rep. Bishop emailed him telling him not to 'cave in to the Politically Correct Taliban! Y'all should have all of the sane states to coordinate and pass these bills on the same day so one state does not have to stand up to these pompous asses alone.' Rep. Bishop replied, 'I LOVE that idea. Taliban. Love that too. Not giving up. Ever.' The CBJ also revealed that 'a separate exchange with another supporter included a declaration by the lawmaker that 'the LGBT movement jeopardizes freedom.'" Human Rights Campaign, "New Emails Reveal North Carolina HB2 Author Compared LGBTQ Advocates to Taliban," *The Gayly* (June 10, 2016), https://www.gayly.com/new-emails-reveal-north-carolina-hb2-author-compared-lgbtq-advocates-taliban.

21. David Badash, "'I Don't Fear Man. I Fear God.': Email Reveals HB2 Has Some Religious Roots," *The New Civil Rights Movement*, June 10, 2016, https://www.thenewcivilrightsmovement.com/2016/06/hb2_author_dan_bishop_i_don_t_fear_man_i_fear_god/.

22. "Alliance Defending Freedom," Southern Poverty Law Center, https://www.splcenter.org/fighting-hate/extremist-files/group/alliance-defending-freedom.

23. Zack Ford, "Is Alliance Defending Freedom a Hate Group? Just Look at Their Work," *ThinkProgress* (August 18, 2018), https://archive.thinkprogress.org/adf-hate-group-3302dd95ace4/; "Dan Bishop's Harsh History of Discrimination," *Charlotte Observer* (August 15, 2019).

24. WCNC Staff, "NC Files Lawsuit against Federal Government over HB2," *KSDK.com* (May 9, 2016), https://www.ksdk.com/article/news/local/nc-files-lawsuit-against-federal-government-over-hb2/275-182367270.

25. Elizabeth Baier and Jeff Tiberii, "HB2: How Did We Get Here?" *WUNC*

(March 23, 2017), https://www.wunc.org/politics/2017-03-23/hb2-how-did-we-get-here.

26. Mark Binker, "Newton Says Dems 'A Little Sensitive' in Reaction to HB2 Comment," *WRAL* (April 26, 2016), https://www.wral.com/newton-says-dems-a-little-sensitive-in-reaction-to-hb2-comment/15665696/.

27. Elizabeth Leland, "Permission to Hate," *Charlotte Observer* (2016), https://www.charlotteobserver.com/news/special-reports/permission-to-hate/.

28. Jason Husser, Kaye Usry, and Owen Covington, "North Carolina Voters on Election 2020 Issues: Views of the Economy, Healthcare, and the Political System," Elon University (2020), https://eloncdn.blob.core.windows.net/eu3/sites/819/2020/02/2020_2_26-ElonPoll_Report_final.pdf.

29. See Carol E. Lee and Amanda Hayes, "Fight for Evangelical Voters Could Be Critical in North Carolina," *NBC News* (November 2, 2020).

30. Gene Demby and Shereen Marisol Meraji, "The White Elephants in the Room," *NPR* (November 18, 2020); Myriam Renaud, "Myths Debunked: Why Did White Evangelicals Vote for Trump?" *The University of Chicago Divinity School* (January 19, 2017); Harriet Sherwood, "Christians Voted for Donald Trump over Hillary Clinton," *The Guardian*, April 2020; David Brooks, "The Dissenters Trying to Save Evangelicalism from Itself," *New York Times* (February 4, 2022); Molly Worthen, "A Match Made in Heaven," *The Atlantic* (May 2017).

31. Demby and Meraji, "The White Elephants in the Room." See also Robert P. Jones, "Racism among White Christians Is Higher than among the Nonreligious. That's no Coincidence," *NBC News* (July 27, 2020), https://www.nbcnews.com/think/opinion/racism-among-white-christians-higher-among-nonreligious-s-no-coincidence-ncna1235045.

32. See Robert P. Jones, *White Too Long: The Legacy of White Supremacy in American Christianity* (Simon & Schuster, 2020); Tom Gjelten, "White Supremacist Ideas Have Historical Roots in Christianity," *NPR* (July 1, 2020), https://www.wuft.org/nation-world/2020/07/01/white-supremacist-ideas-have-historical-roots-in-u-s-christianity/.

33. Demby and Meraji, *supra* note 30.

34. See Eliza Griswold, "God, Guns, and Country: The Evangelical Fight over Firearms," *The New Yorker* (April 19, 2019), https://www.newyorker.com/news/on-religion/god-guns-and-country-the-evangelical-fight-over-firearms; Neil J. Young, "Why Do Evangelicals Oppose Gun Control?" *The Week* (August 11, 2019), https://theweek.com/articles/857806/why-evangelicals-oppose-gun-control.

35. Nicholas Kristof, "Progressive Christians Arise! Hallelujah!" *New York*

Times (March 20, 2021), https://www.nytimes.com/2021/03/20/opinion/sunday /progressive-christians-politics.html (quoting Rev. William Barber).

36. Matt. 5:1–48, 6:1–34, 7:1–29.

37. Frederick Douglass, *Narrative of the Life of Frederick Douglass, an American Slave* (Anti-Slavery Office, 1845).

38. Gjelten, *supra* note 32.

39. Raymond Arsenault, *Freedom Riders: 1961 and the Struggle for Racial Justice* (Oxford University Press, 2007). See also Terry Gross, "Get on the Bus: The Freedom Riders of 1961," *NPR* (January 12, 2006), https://www.npr.org /2006/01/12/5149667/get-on-the-bus-the-freedom-riders-of-1961.

40. Gjelten, *supra* note 32. See also Alan Cross, *When Heaven and Earth Collide: Racism, Southern Evangelicals, and the Better Way of Jesus* (NewSouth Books, 2014).

41. See also analogous arguments concerning Christian nationalists' role in the January 6 insurrection. But it makes a glimmer of sense once you understand that their allegiance is to a belief in blood, earth, and religion rather than to the mere idea of a government "of the people, by the people, for the people." Katherine Stewart, "Christian Nationalism Is One of Trump's Most Powerful Weapons," *New York Times* (January 6, 2022), https://www.nytimes.com/2022/01/06/opinion /jan-6-christian-nationalism.html.

42. I explained my decision this way: "The display of a Christian cross in the heart of our most important building sends an unmistakable message that the chapel belongs more fully to some of us than to others. That there are, at the College, insiders and outsiders. Those for whom our most revered place is meant to be keenly welcoming, and those for whom presence is only tolerated. That distinction, I believe, to be contrary to the best values of the College." See Gene Nichol, "Establishing Inequality," *Michigan Law Review* 107, issue 6 (2009): 913, 926–9; Ira C. Lupu and Robert W. Tuttle, "The Cross at College: Accommodation and Acknowledgment of Religion at Public Universities," *William & Mary Bill of Rights Journal* 16, issue 4 (2008): 939, 955.

43. Nichol, *supra* note 42; Lupu and Tuttle, *supra* note 42.

44. Nichol, *supra* note 42 at 929.

45. Ibid. at 929–30.

46. Ibid. at 928–30.

Chapter 3

1. Laura Leslie, "Lawmakers Debate Whether Schools Should Continue Providing Free Meals to All Students," *WRAL* (February 9, 2022).

2. Ibid. See also Editorial, "North Carolina Must Do More for Food Insecure Children," *Daily Tar Heel* (February 14, 2022), https://www.dailytarheel.com /article/2022/02/opinion-nc-child-hunger.

3. Editorial, *supra* note 2.

4. Gene Nichol, *Indecent Assembly: The North Carolina Legislature's Blueprint for the War on Democracy and Equality* (Blair, 2019), ch. 3.

5. Adam Searing, "Senator Burr on Kids: Hogs at the Trough," *NC Policy Watch* (February 16, 2009).

6. Brian Beutler, "A GOP Senate Candidate Blows the Lid off Conservative Racial Politics," *The New Republic* (May 6, 2014).

7. Peter Holley, "Congressman: Charlotte Protestors 'Hate White People Because White People Are Successful,'" *Washington Post* (September 23, 2016).

8. Lynn Bonner, "North Carolina Begins Drug Testing for Welfare Applicants," *Raleigh News & Observer* (February 10, 2016); Ned Barnett, "Drug Tests Dispel a Myth about North Carolina's Poor," *Raleigh News & Observer* (February 22, 2016).

9. Nichol, *supra* note 4 at ch. 10.

10. Alexander Jones, "Kicking the Unemployed When They're Down," *PoliticsNC* (September 2, 2015).

11. Rob Schofield, "Cutting Food Assistance to the Poor? Really??" *NC Policy Watch* (October 6, 2015).

12. Saki Knafo, "George Cleveland, Republican Rep., Claims No Extreme Poverty in North Carolina as Preschool Cuts Weighed," *Huffington Post* (March 2, 2012).

13. Ibid. See also "Onslow County, NC," Census Reporter, https://census reporter.org/profiles/05000US37133-onslow-county-nc/.

14. Gene Nichol, *The Faces of Poverty in North Carolina: Stories from Our Invisible Citizens* (University of North Carolina Press, 2018), 1–10.

15. See John Cassidy, "Piketty's Inequality Story in Six Charts," *New Yorker* (March 26, 2014), https://www.newyorker.com/news/john-cassidy/pikettys -inequality-story-in-six-charts; Nichol, *supra* note 4 at ch. 3.

16. See Gene Nichol and Heather Hunt, "The Persistent and Pervasive Challenge of Child Poverty and Hunger in North Carolina," *NC Poverty Research Fund* (December 2021), https://law.unc.edu/wp-content/uploads/2021/12/NC-child -poverty_final-web.pdf.

17. "Alston, Philip; UN Human Rights Council. Special Rapporteur on Extreme Poverty and Human Rights," United Nations Digital Library, https://digitallibrary .un.org/record/3883131.

18. Nichol and Hunt, *supra* note 16.

19. Ibid.

20. Ibid. See also Nichol, *supra* note 14 at 26–39.

21. Nichol, *supra* note 14 at ch. 2.

22. Ibid.

23. Heather Hunt and Gene Nichol, "'Surviving through Together': Hunger, Poverty and Persistence in High Point, North Carolina," *NC Poverty Research Fund* (Fall 2019), 43, https://law.unc.edu/wp-content/uploads/2019/12/High-Point -12102019-web.pdf.

24. Nichol, *supra* note 14 at 26–28.

25. Ibid. at 84–85.

26. Ibid. at 169.

27. Ibid. at 48–49.

28. Ava Kofman, "How North Carolina Transformed Itself into the Worst State to Be Unemployed," *ProPublica* (June 30, 2020), https://www.propublica .org/article/how-north-carolina-transformed-itself-into-the-worst-state-to-be -unemployed; Gene Nichol, "NC's Unemployment Pay Cuts Hurt Now," *Raleigh News & Observer* (April 13, 2020).

29. Nichol, *supra* note 28. See also Gene Nichol, "Amid Virus, GOP Punishes the Poor," *Raleigh News & Observer* (May 5, 2020); Catherine New, "North Carolina Unemployment Benefit Cuts Harshest in the Country: Report," *HuffPost* (February 11, 2013), https://www.huffpost.com/entry/north-carolina-unemployment -benefits-cuts_n_2662511?guccounter=1&guce_referrer=aHR0cHM6Ly93d3cu YmluZy5jb20v&guce_referrer_sig=AQAAAGc2sxv5m1eiGFjjqG3U7vr78xh -xUubgERwYInkVBqK_RdbVAnw1azmIkn1Vb5Aab05M1bc-QDYwWhoMRPEcw OERcFr92glwX7AERt0r077mLycbalpT5cn0lKYGWJCgqs0c4IOemzwd0 PVpP2ZQMEZLb11k8Q6TdoM4vFxhcWg; Sophie Kasakove, "Unemployment Appeals Backlog in NC Leaves Many Waiting," *Raleigh News & Observer* (January 13, 2021).

30. Editorial, "The Decline of North Carolina," *New York Times* (July 9, 2013).

31. Allyson M. Corbo, Sara Y. Correa, Rosa Greenberg, Paige Logan, and Heather Hunt, "Violence against the Poor: The Consequences of North Carolina's Failure to Expand Medicaid," *NC Poverty Research Fund* (May 2020), https:// s39248.p1438.sites.pressdns.com/wp-content/uploads/2020/06/Violence -Against-the-Poor-Medicaid-Expansion-report.pdf. See also "Report: NC's Failure to Expand Medicaid Constitutes 'Violence against the Poor,'" *NC Policy Watch* (June 4, 2020), https://ncpolicywatch.com/2020/06/04/report-ncs-failure-to -expand-medicaid-constitutes-violence-against-the-poor/.

32. See Nichol, *supra* note 4 at 36–39.

33. Ibid. at 37.

34. Ibid. at 36–40; Chris Fitzsimon, "The Ways Regressive Tax Hikes Will Hurt NC Poor," *Raleigh News & Observer* (September 18, 2015); Alexandra Forter Sirota, "State Budget Agreement Doubles Down Once More on Regressive Tax Policies," *NC Policy Watch* (June 29, 2016).

35. Nichol, *supra* note 4 at 31–50.

36. Editorial, *supra* note 30; Michael Fletcher, "An Unimpeded GOP Veers North Carolina to the Right," *Washington Post* (May 20, 2013); Jason Zengerle, "Is North Carolina the Future of American Politics?" *New York Times Magazine* (June 20, 2017), quoting Rob Christensen; Karen Cox, "What's the Matter with North Carolina?" *New York Times* (December 19, 2016).

37. Nichol, *supra* note 4 at 31–36.

38. Stan Dorn, "The COVID-19 Pandemic and Resulting Economic Crash Have Caused the Greatest Health Insurance Losses in American History," *Families USA* (July 13, 2020), https://www.familiesusa.org/wp-content/uploads/2020/07/COV-254_Coverage-Loss_Report_7-14-20.pdf. See also Nichol, *supra* note 14 at afterword.

39. Dorn, *supra* note 38. See also Rob Schofield, "Report: NC is Fifth in the Nation in Lost Health Insurance Coverage Due to the Covid-19 Recession," *NC Policy Watch* (July 16, 2020), http://pulse.ncpolicywatch.org/2020/07/16/report-nc-is-fifth-in-the-nation-in-lost-health-insurance-coverage-due-to-the-covid-19-recession/#sthash.bNymN6xS.dpbs.

40. Nichol, *supra* note 14 at afterword, 175–85.

41. See Schofield, *supra* note 39.

42. See Steve Ford, "The Virus and the Vulnerable," *NC Policy Watch* (August 3, 2020), http://www.ncpolicywatch.com/2020/08/03/the-virus-and-the-vulnerable/.

43. See Nichol, *supra* note 14 at afterword, 175–85.

44. Ibid. at afterword, 181–83.

45. Brown v. Board of Education of Topeka, 347 U.S. 473 (1954); Gene Nichol, "Richmond Bar Association Law Day Address," College of William & Mary, Williamsburg, V.A. (May 1, 2007), https://www.wm.edu/about/administration/president/office-contacts-history/history/twentyone/nichol/addresses/richmondbar/index.php.

46. Rev. Dr. William J. Barber II, "The Sermon," Washington National Cathedral, Washington, D.C. (June 14, 2020), https://cathedral.org/sermons/sermon-the-rev-dr-william-j-barber-ii-2/; April Ryan, "Rev. Dr. Barber: Refuse to Be Comfortable with the Death of Others," *American Urban Radio Networks* (April 23, 2020), https://aurn.com/rev-dr-barber-refuse-to-be-comfortable-with-the-death-of-others/.

Chapter 4

1. William Myers, "Hark the Sound," arrangement by Earl Slocum (1897), https://library.unc.edu/music/uncsongs/. "Hark the sound of Tar Heels' voices, Ringing clear and true, Singing Carolina's praises, Shouting NCU. Hail to the brightest star of all, Clear its radiance shine, Carolina priceless gem, Receive all praises thine."

2. Erin Baucom, "What Is It That Binds Us to This Speech? Charles Kuralt's 1993 UNC Bicentennial Address," *UNC University Libraries* (January 26, 2016), https://blogs.lib.unc.edu/uarms/2016/01/26/what-is-it-that-binds-us-to-this-speech-charles-kuralts-1993-unc-bicentennial-address/.

3. Ibid.

4. See Gene Nichol, "Losing Carolina," *Southern Cultures* 25, no. 1 (Spring 2019): 106–23.

5. Ibid.

6. Patty Courtright, "Brief Encounter Leads to 100 Years of Women at Carolina," *UNC News Services* (October 10, 1997), https://www.unc.edu/news/archives/oct97/100.html (site discontinued).

7. Counsel for the plaintiffs were Thurgood Marshall and Robert L. Carter with Conrad Pearson of Durham, N.C., on the brief. McKissick v. Carmichael, 187 F.2d 949 (4th Cir.), *cert. denied*, 341 U.S. 951 (1951). See also Charles E. Daye, "(Sesquicentennial) African-American and Other Minority Law Students and Alumni," *North Carolina Law Review* 73 (1995): 675, http://scholarship.law.unc.edu/nclr/vol73/iss2/18.

8. L. J. Toler, "Carolina Celebrates Fifty Years of African-American Students," *UNC News Services* (November 27, 2001), http://www.unc.edu/news/archives/nov01/bsm112601.htm (site discontinued).

9. "First Black Undergraduate Students," The Carolina Story: A Virtual Museum of University History, https://museum.unc.edu/exhibits/show/integration/leroy-frasier--john-lewis-bran.

10. See Rachel Gogal and Rob Holliday, "Honoring an Unsung Legacy," *University Communications* (February 27, 2017), https://www.unc.edu/discover/honoring-unsung-legacy/.

11. See Geeta N. Kapur, *To Drink from the Well: The Struggle for Racial Equality at the Nation's Oldest Public University* (Blair, 2021), introduction.

12. Ibid.

13. Gene Nichol, "Johnston County School Rule Would Bar Reading of UNC Court Decision," *Raleigh News & Observer* (October 28, 2021), https://www.newsobserver.com/opinion/article255296946.html#storylink=cpy.

14. See Nichol, *supra* note 4.

15. Ibid.; "Wayne J. Urban," Louise McBee Institute of Higher Education, https://ihe.uga.edu/directory/people/wayne-j-urban. Wayne Urban is a professor emeritus at the University of Alabama and a regents' professor emeritus at Georgia State University. After a long career at Georgia State University, Urban spent ten years as a professor of higher education at the University of Alabama. While there, he coordinated the Higher Education Administration Program and served as associate director of the Education Policy Center.

16. Nichol, *supra* note 4.

17. William Snider, *Light on the Hill: A History of the University of North Carolina at Chapel Hill* (University of North Carolina Press, 1992), 7 (citing *N.C. Const.* art. XLI).

18. Ibid. at 10.

19. Ibid. at 11.

20. William S. Powell, *North Carolina through Four Centuries* (University of North Carolina Press, 1989), 216.

21. Ibid. at 23 (quoting David Lively).

22. See Michael A. Cooper Jr., "The War on the War on Poverty," *The New Republic* (February 15, 2015).

23. See Nichol, *supra* note 4.

24. Ibid.

25. Ibid.

26. "Report of a Special Committee: Governance, Academic Freedom, and Institutional Racism in the University of North Carolina System," American Association of University Professors (April 2022).

27. Ibid.

28. Dawn Baumgardner, "Fast Moving Bill Would Shift Control of College Boards," *Raleigh News & Observer* (June 12, 2022), https://www.newsobserver.com/news/politics-government/article262306372.html.

29. Dawn Baumgardner, "Tom Ross Asked to Leave UNC System Presidency," *Raleigh News & Observer* (January 16, 2015), https://www.newsobserver.com/news/local/education/article10223801.html.

30. The interactions leading to the closure of the poverty center have been much documented in the press (see the citations in the piece below, where my arguments are laid out more completely).

31. To be absurdly brief, the North Carolina General assembly eliminated 460,000 poor people from the Medicaid rolls, ushering in the largest cut to an unemployment compensation program ever, abolishing the state earned income tax

credit, slashing child care and housing subsidies, kicking hundreds of thousands of eligible recipients off food stamps, eliminating the state appropriation for legal aid, dramatically reducing available subsidies for childhood dental services, requiring drug tests for public benefits, and substantially raising sales taxes so that poor residents pay proportionally more to the tax man—as taxes were dramatically reduced for the wealthiest 2 percent of taxpayers. See Gene Nichol, *The Faces of Poverty in North Carolina: Stories from Our Invisible Citizens* (University of North Carolina Press, 2018), ch. 10.

32. Ibid.

33. Ibid.

34. Ibid.

35. Gene Nichol, "Lessons on Political Speech, Academic Freedom, and University Governance from the New North Carolina," *First Amendment Law Review* (2018), 50.

36. Ibid.

37. Jane Stancill, "UNC Law School Budget Cut by North Carolina Legislators," *Raleigh News & Observer* (June 20, 2017), https://www.newsobserver.com/news/local/education/article157121589.html. See also Nichol, *supra* note 35.

38. See American Association of University Professors, *supra* note 26.

39. The Poverty Center was closed by the Board of Governors on July 1, 2015. That same day, with the help of a supportive dean (Jack Boger), we opened the UNC School of Law's new North Carolina Poverty Research Fund. Donors who had supported the initial poverty center transferred grants and donations to the research fund. Thankfully, many new and unsolicited contributions were received from North Carolinians who were outraged by the acts of legislative censorship. So the work of the original poverty center was continued, with the same staff and students, with modestly more insulation from the overreach of the Board of Governors and with additional resources. I also, of course, kept publishing articles in the *News & Observer* and the *Charlotte Observer*. Two weeks earlier, in the closing days of the legislative session, Senate Republican leaders, without notice or debate, inserted an amendment into the final Senate budget cutting $3 million from the UNC School of Law. Democrats protested from the floor that the move was political payback for the school's "employment of legislative critic Gene Nichol." When one dissenter asked whether any other schools or agencies should be prepared for such arbitrary reductions, the Senate sponsor said, simply, "No." State Sen. Mike Woodard objected that this was nothing more than "the Gene Nichol transfer amendment." The budget cut passed easily, along party lines. It was, however, removed in confer-

ence with the House. In June 2017, legislators took more wounding steps. Again, at the close of the budgeting process, the Senate introduced a previously undisclosed cut to the UNC School of Law's budget—this time $4 million, or about 30 percent of the total state appropriation. Newspapers across North Carolina said the revision was seemingly aimed "squarely" at legislative critic Gene Nichol. They argued that the General Assembly should "have nothing to fear from a professor who speaks his mind." The dean of the state's political columnists, Rob Cristensen, said the Republican legislators were sending a message carved with a "chain saw." The message, unsurprisingly, was that they "[don't] like Gene Nichol." In conference with the House, the cut was reduced from $4 million to $500,000 and then passed. Newspapers opined that the arbitrary cut was outrageous but "could have been worse." Expectations are now very low in North Carolina. See Nichol, *supra* note 35.

40. Ibid.

41. Jane Stancill, "UNC Civil Rights Center Litigation Ban," *Durham Herald Sun* (July 27, 2017), https://www.heraldsun.com/news/local/education/article 163939422.html; Nichol, *supra* note 35.

42. See American Association of University Professors, *supra* note 26; Nichol, *supra* note 35.

43. American Association of University Professors, *supra* note 26.

44. Nichol, *supra* note 35.

45. Ibid.

46. Joe Killian, "UNC Press Now in the Crosshairs of Board of Governors, Which Is Refusing to Re-appoint Professor Who Criticized Handling of Silent Sam Monument," *NC Policy Watch* (June 21, 2021), https://ncpolicywatch.com/2021/06/21 /unc-press-now-in-the-crosshairs-of-board-of-governors-which-is-refusing-to-re -appoint-professor-who-criticized-handling-of-silent-sam-moment/.

47. Ibid.; see American Association of University Professors, *supra* note 26.

48. See American Association of University Professors, *supra* note 26.

49. See Joe Killian, "Email Trove Reveals New Details of UNC Board of Governors' Refusal to Reappoint Popular UNC Press Board Chair," *NC Policy Watch* (March 31, 2022), https://ncpolicywatch.com/2022/03/31/email-trove-reveals -new-details-of-unc-board-of-governors-refusal-to-reappoint-popular-unc-press -board-chair/?eType=EmailBlastContent&eId=120d96e8-c991-48e4-8d90-4ac977 b3859c.

50. Ibid.; see Gene Nichol, "UNC Overseers Punish Outspoken Law Professor," *Raleigh News & Observer* (June 23, 2021), https://www.newsobserver.com/opinion /article252305893.html.

51. Gene Nichol, "The Latest Political Pillaging of NC's Flagship University," *Charlotte Observer* (May 28, 2021), https://www.charlotteobserver.com/opinion/article251719208.html.

52. Ibid.; see American Association of University Professors, *supra* note 26.

53. American Association of University Professors, *supra* note 26.

54. Ibid.

55. Ibid. at 8.

56. Ibid.

57. Ibid. at 9.

58. Ibid.

59. See Gene Nichol, "Faculty Empowerment in the Threatened UNC System," Appalachian State University, Boone, N.C. (April 28, 2022), https://drive.google.com/file/d/1JssMun_200LbfYaU4lMzyPhaY_XpP1Le/view.

60. Ibid. at 18.

61. Mimi Chapman, "Op-ed: UNC Chancellor Is Facing Pressure for New Provost Decision," *Daily Tar Heel* (December 2021).

62. Ibid.; see Special Report of the AAUP outlining appointment controversies at Fayetteville State, East Carolina, Appalachian State, and Western Carolina universities.

63. See American Association of University Professors, *supra* note 26. See also Adway S. Wadekar, "'Political Meddling from on High': AAUP, Faculty Condemn University of North Carolina System Leadership," *The Chronicle* (June 21, 2022), https://www.dukechronicle.com/article/2022/06/university-of-north-carolina-system-american-association-of-university-professors-faculty-governance-academic-freedom.

64. "UNC System: 'Pervasive and Overtly Partisan Political Control,'" Higher Ed Works, https://www.higheredworks.org/2022/05/unc-system-pervasive-and-overtly-partisan-political-control/; Kate Murphy, "UNC–Chapel Hill Journalism School Faces Accreditation Threat," *Raleigh News & Observer* (May 2, 2022), https://www.newsobserver.com/news/local/education/article260983112.html Diversity; Ava Pukatch, "'Black Eye on UNC System': National Group Considers Sanctions," *Chapelboro.com* (May 4, 2022), https://chapelboro.com/news/unc/black-eye-on-unc-system-national-group-considers-sanctions; American Association of University Professors, *supra* note 26. See also Caitlyn Yaede, "Column: Hussman's Provisional Accreditation Is Not 'Unexpected,'" *Daily Tar Heel* (May 4, 2022), https://www.dailytarheel.com/article/2022/05/opinion-hussman-school-downgraded-accreditation.

65. Karin Fischer, "The Red-State Disadvantage," *Chronicle of Higher Educa-*

tion (February 11, 2022). See also Daniel Golden and Kirsten Berg, "The Red State University Blues," *Chronicle of Higher Education* (June 29, 2022), https://www.chronicle.com/article/the-red-state-university-blues?utm_source=Iterable&utm_medium=email&utm_campaign=campaign_4564792_nl_Academe-Today_date_20220629&cid=at&source=&sourceid=&cid2=gen_login_refresh.

66. Fischer, *supra* note 65.

67. That is the conclusion of the American Association of University Professors. Kate Murphy, "AAUP Report Shows Politics Threatens Academic Freedom at UNC," *Raleigh News & Observer* (April 28, 2022), https://www.newsobserver.com/news/local/education/article260820252.html#storylink=mainstage_card5; Joe Killian, "National Faculty Organization Releases Scathing Report on UNC System," *NC Policy Watch* (April 28, 2022); Stephanie Saul, "G.O.P. Lawmakers Subverted U. of North Carolina, Professors' Group Says," *New York Times* (April 28, 2022), https://www.nytimes.com/2022/04/28/us/unc-report-gop.html.

68. Snider, *supra* note 17 at 188.

69. Gene Nichol, "Bill Aycock and the North Carolina Speaker Ban Law," *North Carolina Law Review* 79 (2001): 1725.

70. James Moeser, *The State of the University, 2000–2008: Major Addresses by UNC Chancellor James Moeser* (University of North Carolina Press, 2018), 23.

71. Ibid at 23–47, 53.

Chapter 5

1. Yasmeen Abutaleb, Cleve R. Wootson Jr., and Marianna Sotomayor, "Frustration, Anger Rising among Democrats over Caution on Abortion," *Washington Post* (June 27, 2022).

2. See Gene Nichol, *Indecent Assembly: The North Carolina Legislature's Blueprint for the War on Democracy and Equality* (Blair, 2019); Karen Cox, "What's the Matter with North Carolina?" *New York Times* (December 19, 2016); David A. Graham, "How North Carolina Became the Wisconsin of 2013," *The Atlantic* (July 1, 2013), https://www.theatlantic.com/politics/archive/2013/07/how-north-carolina-became-the-wisconsin-of-2013/277007/.

3. Cox, *supra* note 2.

4. Gene Nichol, "In N.C.—One of the Hungriest States—A Call to Cut Food Stamps," *Raleigh News & Observer* (May 25, 2017), https://www.newsobserver.com/opinion/op-ed/article152432659.html; Gene Nichol, "Government Sponsored Religion at NC Crisis Pregnancy Centers," *Charlotte Observer* (July 1, 2019), https://www.charlotteobserver.com>article232068072.

5. Graham, *supra* note 2.

6. Cox, *supra* note 2.

7. See Aaron Sánchez-Guerra, "Moral Monday Returns to Raleigh to Call for Social Reform," *Raleigh News & Observer* (March 29, 2022). See also "The Dynamics of Moral Mondays: A Human Rights Movement," *PopularResistance.org* (February 13, 2014).

8. See Sánchez-Guerra, *supra* note 7; Rev. Dr. William J. Barber II and Jonathan Wilson-Hartgrove, *The Third Reconstruction: How a Moral Movement Is Overcoming the Politics of Division and Fear* (Beacon Press, 2016).

9. Barber and Wilson-Hartgrove, *supra* note 8 at 73–109. See also Cleve R. Wootson Jr., "Rev. William Barber Builds a Moral Movement," *Washington Post* (June 29, 2017), https://www.washingtonpost.com/news/acts-of-faith/wp/2017/06/29/woe-unto-those-who-legislate-evil-rev-william-barber-builds-a-moral-movement/.

10. Sánchez-Guerra, *supra* note 7.

11. Barber and Wilson-Hartgrove, *supra* note 8 at 101. See also Nichol, *supra* note 2 at x–xvi (foreword by Reverend Barber and Dr. Timothy Tyson).

12. Barber and Wilson-Hartgrove, *supra* note 8 at 100–111.

13. See "The Dynamics of Moral Mondays," *supra* note 7.

14. Barber and Wilson-Hartgrove, *supra* note 8.

15. Ibid. at 122.

16. Gene Nichol, *The Faces of Poverty in North Carolina: Stories from Our Invisible Citizens* (University of North Carolina Press, 2018), 184–85 ("Afterword: A National Poor People's Movement").

17. Barber and Wilson-Hartgrove, *supra* note 8.

18. Ibid. at 105–6.

19. Ibid. at 104–5.

20. Ibid. at 104.

21. Ibid. at 104–5.

22. See, particularly, Nichol, *supra* note 2.

23. The Rolling Stones, "Sympathy for the Devil," track 1 on *Beggars Banquet*, Decca Records (1968).

24. "Michigan State Senator Fights Back against 'Hateful Garbage,'" *The Norman Transcript* (April 2022), https://www.normantranscript.com/region/michigan-state-senator-gains-national-spotlight-pushing-back-against-hateful-garbage/article_c855d67e-c3c4-5093-bfdb-483e71098d52.html. See also Blake Hounshell, "Smeared as a Groomer, a Michigan Democrat Goes on Offense," *New York Times* (April 25, 2022); PBS NewsHour, "WATCH: Michigan Lawmaker Says, 'We Will Not Let Hate Win,'" YouTube (April 20, 2022), https://www.youtube.com

/watch?v=iLWo8BiRoMY; Frances Kai-Hwa Wang, "'We Will Not Let Hate Win,' Michigan Lawmaker Says," *PBS* (April 22, 2022), https://www.pbs.org/newshour /politics/watch-michigan-lawmaker-says-we-will-not-let-hate-win.

25. Hounshell, *supra* note 24.

26. Gene Nichol and Heather Hunt, "Goldsboro: Isolation and Marginalization in Eastern North Carolina," *North Carolina Research Fund* (Winter 2018). See also "Isolation and Marginalization in Eastern North Carolina," *NC Policy Watch* (January 29, 2018), https://ncpolicywatch.com/2018/01/29/isolation -marginalization-eastern-north-carolina/.

27. Nichol and Hunt, *supra* note 26.

28. Ibid.

29. Gene Nichol and Heather Hunt, "Mountain Poverty and Resilience," *North Carolina Poverty Research Fund* (Summer 2017), https://www2.law.unc.edu/ documents/poverty/publications/wilkes_report_web.pdf.

30. Ibid.

31. Ibid.

32. Gene Nichol, "In NC's Struggling Regions: 'Folks Feel Like They've Had the Hell Kicked out of Them,'" *Raleigh News & Observer* (March 29, 2018), https:// www.newsobserver.com/opinion/op-ed/article207260424.html; Nichol, *supra* note 16.

33. W. J. Cash, *The Mind of the South* (Alfred A. Knopf, 1941); Bob Dylan, "Only a Pawn in Their Game," track 1 on *The Times They Are A-Changin'*, Columbia Records (1964), https://www.bobdylan.com/songs/only-pawn-their-game/.

Chapter 6

1. Brown v. Board of Education of Topeka, 347 U.S. 483 (1954) (declaring that the "separate but equal" doctrine has no place in determining equal educational rights under the Fourteenth Amendment).

2. See Loving v. Virginia, 388 U.S.1 (1967) (interracial marriage); Reed v. Reed, 404 U.S. 71 (1971) (sex discrimination); Graham v. Richardson, 403 U.S. 365 (1966) (state discrimination against noncitizens).

3. See Duncan v. Louisiana, 391 U.S. 145 (1968).

4. See Harper v. Virginia Board of Elections, 383 U.S. 663 (1966) (poll tax); Reynolds v. Sims, 377 U.S. 533 (1964) (redistricting).

5. See New York Times Co. v. Sullivan, 376 U.S. 254 (1964) (libel); New York Times Co. v. United States, 403 U.S. 713 (1971) (no prior restraint); Brandenburg v. Ohio, 395 U.S. 444 (1969) (bolstering the clear and present danger test).

6. See Sherbert v. Verner, 374 U.S. 398 (1963) (free exercise).

7. See Shapiro v. Thompson, 394 U.S. 618 (1969) (travel).

8. See Fuentes v. Shevin, 407 U.S. 67 (1972) (right to preseizure hearing).

9. See Burton v. Wilmington Parking Authority, 365 U.S. 715 (1961).

10. See Griswold v. Connecticut, 381 U.S. 479 (1965) (contraceptive use by married couples).

11. Roe v. Wade, 410 U.S. 113 (1973) (abortion); Miranda v. Arizona, 384 U.S. 436 (1966) (confessions); Regents of the University of California v. Bakke, 438 U.S. 265 (1978).

12. John Hart Ely, *Democracy and Distrust: A Theory of Judicial Review* (Harvard University Press, 1980).

13. Paul N. Cox, "John Hart Ely, Democracy and Distrust: A Theory of Judicial Review," *Valparaiso University Law Review* 15, no. 3 (1981): 637.

14. Ely, *supra* note 12.

15. See Gene Nichol, *Indecent Assembly: The North Carolina Legislature's Blueprint for the War on Democracy and Equality* (Blair, 2019).

16. Covington v. North Carolina, 316 F.R.D. 117 (M.D.N.C., 2016).

17. Ibid.

18. Covington v. North Carolina, 270 F. Supp. 3d at 881 (2017).

19. Ibid. at 884.

20. Ibid. at 891.

21. Ibid. at 891–7.

22. Ibid. at 896.

23. Common Cause v. Rucho, 318 F. Supp. 3d 777 (M.D.N.C. 2018), vacated 139 S. Ct. 2484 (2019).

24. Ibid. at 933–44.

25. Dickinson v. Rucho, 368 N.C. 481, 491 (2015), vacated 137 S. Ct. 2186 (2017).

26. *Common Cause v. Rucho* was eventually reversed by the United States Supreme Court on jurisdictional grounds, deeming it a political question. See Common Cause v. Rucho, 588 US (2019). The three-judge court decision appears at Common Cause v. Rucho, 279 F. Supp. 3d 587 (M.D.N.C. 2018). The North Carolina state courts, however, used the theory of the three-judge court to invalidate extreme political gerrymandering under the state constitution of North Carolina. Rucho v. Common Cause, 138 S. Ct. 2679 (2018). See Common Cause v. Lewis, (2019); Joseph Ax, "North Carolina Court Strikes Down State Legislative Map as Unconstitutional Gerrymander," *Reuters* (September 3, 2019), https://www.reuters .com/article/us-north-carolina-gerrymandering-idUSKCN1VO2MD; Ally Mutnick, "North Carolina Supreme Court Strikes Down GOP-Drawn Congressional

Map," *Politico* (February 4, 2022), https://www.politico.com/news/2022/02/04/north-carolina-congressional-map-struck-down-00005974.

27. Shelby County v. Holder, 570 U.S. 529 (2013); Brnovich v. Democratic National Committee, 594 U.S. (2021), no. 19-1257; Nina Totenberg, "The Supreme Court Deals a New Blow to Voting Rights, Upholding Arizona Restrictions," *NPR* (July 1, 2021), https://www.npr.org/2021/07/01/998758022/the-supreme-court-up.

28. Brnovich v. Democratic National Committee, *supra* note 27 (Justice Kagan dissenting).

29. Rucho v. Common Cause, 588 U.S. (2019), No. 18-422.

30. Michael Wines, "North Carolina Court Says G.O.P. Political Maps Violate State Constitution," *New York Times* (February 4, 2022), https://www.nytimes.com/2022/02/04/us/north-carolina-redistricting-gerrymander-unconstitutional.html.

31. See Robert Barnes, "Supreme Court to Review State Legislatures' Power in Federal Elections, *Washington Post* (June 30, 2022), https://www.washingtonpost.com/politics/2022/06/30/supreme-court-federal-elections-state-legislatures/.

32. Adam Liptak and Nick Corasaniti, "Supreme Court to Hear Case on State Legislatures' Power over Elections," *New York Times* (June 30, 2022), https://www.nytimes.com/2022/06/30/us/politics/state-legislatures-elections-supreme-court.html.

33. Gene Nichol, "The U.S. Supreme Court Has Become Politicians in Black Robes," *Raleigh News & Observer* (May 5, 2022), https://www.newsobserver.com/opinion/article261112702.html.

34. Sen. Susan Collins claims that Justice Kavanaugh lied even further: "Start with my record, my respect for precedent, my belief that it is rooted in the Constitution, and my commitment and its importance to the rule of law," he said, according to contemporaneous notes kept by multiple staff members in the meeting. "I understand precedent and I understand the importance of overturning it. Roe is 45 years old, it has been reaffirmed many times, lots of people care about it a great deal, and I've tried to demonstrate I understand real-world consequences," he continued, according to the notes, adding: "I am a don't-rock-the-boat kind of judge. I believe in stability and in the Team of Nine." Ruth Marcus, "Opinion: Susan Collins Needs to Own Up to Her Decision to Back Kavanaugh," *Washington Post* (June 28, 2022).

35. See Dobbs v. Jackson Women's Health Organization, 597 U.S. (2022).

36. Michael H. v. Gerald D., 491 U.S. 110, fn. 6 (1989) (Justice Scalia plurality opinion).

37. Samantha Smith, "Americans Remain Divided on How the Supreme Court Should Interpret the Constitution," *Pew Research Center* (April 6, 2017), https://

www.pewresearch.org/fact-tank/2017/04/06/americans-remain-divided-on-how
-the-supreme-court-should-interpret-the-constitution/.

38. Citizens United v. Federal Election Commission, 558 U.S. 310 (2010).

39. "Thomas Jefferson to George Logan, 12 November 1816," Founders Archives,
https://founders.archives.gov/documents/Jefferson/03-10-02-0390.

40. District of Columbia v. Heller, 554 U.S. 570 (2008) (recognizing the personal
right to possess firearms under the Second Amendment).

41. New York State Rifle & Pistol Association Inc. v. Bruen, 597 U.S. (2022),
https://www.supremecourt.gov/opinions/21pdf/20-843_7j80.pdf. See also Adam
Liptak, "Supreme Court Strikes Down New York Law Limiting Guns in Public," *New York Times* (June 23, 2022), https://www.nytimes.com/2022/06/23/us
/supreme-court-ny-open-carry-gun-law.html.

42. Printz v. United States, 521 U.S. 898 (1997).

43. Adarand Constructors Inc. v. Peña, 515 U.S. 200 (1995).

44. Ibid. (Scalia concurring in part and concurring in the judgment).

45. Shelby County v. Holder, 133 S. Ct. 2612 (2013).

46. Nollan v. California Coastal Commission, 483 U.S. 825 (1987).

47. New York v. United States, 505 U.S. 144 (1992); Printz v. United States, *supra* note 42.

48. National Federation of Independent Business v. Sebelius, 567 U.S. 519 (2012);
United States v. Morrison, 529 U.S. 598 (2000); United States v. Lopez, 514 U.S. at
568, 577.

49. See Dobbs v. Jackson, *supra* note 35, https://www.scotusblog.com/case-files
/cases/dobbs-v-jackson-womens-health-organization/.

50. See Dobbs v. Jackson, *supra* note 35; Kaelan Deese, "READ IN FULL: Supreme Court Decision and Dissent on New York Gun Law," *Washington Exam-
iner* (June 23, 2022), https://www.washingtonexaminer.com/news/justice/read
-in-full-supreme-court-decision-new-york-gun-law.

51. Dred Scott v. Sandford, 60 U.S. (19 How.) 393 (1857) (U.S. constitutional protections do not apply to African Americans).

52. Plessy v. Ferguson, 163 U.S. 537 (1896) (upholding racial apartheid under the
Fourteenth Amendment).

53. Lochner v. New York, 198 U.S. 45 (1905) (invalidating the minimum wage
and maximum hour laws).

54. Buck v. Bell, 274 U.S. 200 (1927).

55. Korematsu v. United States, 323 U.S. 214 (1944) (upholding Japanese American exclusion orders during World War II).

56. San Antonio Independent School District v. Rodriguez, 411 U.S. 1 (1973) (upholding extreme economic discrimination in public education).

57. Bowers v. Hardwick, 478 U.S. 186 (1986) (allowing the criminalization of private, consensual, adult, gay sexual intimacy).

58. Buckley v. Valeo, 424 U.S. 1 (1976) (equating money with speech in elections).

59. See Dobbs v. Jackson, *supra* note 35.

60. Gene Nichol, "Why an Earlier Freedom Ride Still Matters," *Raleigh News & Observer* (May 23, 2022), https://www.newsobserver.com/opinion/article 261704932.html#storylink=cpy.

61. Ibid.

62. Ibid.

63. Raymond Arsenault, *Freedom Riders: 1961 and the Struggle for Racial Justice* (Oxford University Press, 2007).

Chapter 7

1. Abraham Lincoln, "Gettysburg Address," Gettysburg, P.A. (November 19, 1863), https://www.britannica.com/event/Gettysburg-Address.

2. Gene Nichol, "Children of Distant Fathers: Sketching an Ethos of Constitutional Liberty," *Wisconsin Law Review* 1319 (1985).

3. Ibid.

4. Ibid.

5. Ibid.

6. Ibid. See also Rufus Burrow Jr., *Martin Luther King, Jr., and the Theology of Resistance* (McFarland & Company, 2014).

7. Nichol, *supra* note 2.

8. Ibid.

9. Heather Cox Richardson, *Letters from an American*, newsletter published by Substack, https://heathercoxrichardson.substack.com. See also Heather Cox Richardson, *How the South Won the Civil War: Oligarchy, Democracy, and the Continuing Fight for the Soul of America* (Oxford University Press, 2020).

10. See James L. Leloudis and Robert R. Korstad, *Fragile Democracy: The Struggle over Race and Voting Rights in North Carolina* (University of North Carolina Press, 2020).

11. Rebecca Tippett, "NC in Focus: Minority Population Share, 2014," *Carolina Demography* (August 13, 2015), https://www.ncdemography.org/2015/08/1 /nc-in-focus-minority-population-share-2014/.

12. "Cowardly Mark Meadows Allowed January 6 to Happen," *Raleigh News & Observer* (June 29, 2022).

13. Gene Nichol, "Betraying Decency and Democracy in North Carolina," *Facing South* (June 10, 2021).

14. "NC Republicans Amplified Trump's 2020 Election Fraud Lies," *Raleigh News & Observer* (June 13, 2022), https://www.newsobserver.com/opinion/article 262459112.html.

15. Ibid. See also Gene Nichol, "Doubling Down on Sedition," *Raleigh News & Observer* (February 22, 2021).

16. See Gene Nichol, *Indecent Assembly: The North Carolina Legislature's Blueprint for the War on Democracy and Equality* (Blair, 2019), introduction.

17. Cox Richardson, *Letters, supra* note 9.

18. Frederick Douglass, "The Lessons of the Hour," Washington, D.C. (January 9, 1894).

19. Frederick Douglass, "What to the Slave Is the Fourth of July?" Rochester, N.Y. (July 5, 1852); David W. Blight, *Frederick Douglass: Prophet of Freedom* (Simon & Schuster, 2018).

20. Noam Sandweiss-Back, "Lessons from the Greensboro Massacre: Interview with Roz Pelles," *University of the Poor* (2021), https://universityofthepoor.org /lessons-from-the-greensboro-massacre-interview-with-roz-pelles/.

21. Nichol, *supra* note 16 at ch. 1.

22. Dylan Lysen, Laura Ziegler, and Blaise Mesa, "Voters in Kansas Decide to Keep Abortion Legal in the State, Rejecting an Amendment," *NPR* (August 3, 2022), https://www.npr.org/sections/2022-live-primary-election-race-results/2022/08/02 /1115317596/kansas-voters-abortion-legal-reject-constitutional-amendment.

23. See Yascha Mounk, *The Great Experiment: Why Diverse Democracies Fall Apart and How They Can Endure* (Penguin Press, 2022).

24. See Robert F. Kennedy, "Remarks by Attorney General Robert F. Kennedy to the 120th Anniversary Dinner of B'nai B'rith," Chicago, IL (October 13, 1963), https://www.justice.gov/sites/default/files/ag/legacy/2011/01/20/10-13-1963.pdf.

25. See Martin Luther King Jr., "We shall overcome because the arc of the moral universe is long but it bends toward justice." Rev. Dr. Martin Luther King Jr., "Remaining Awake through a Great Revolution," Washington, D.C. (March 31, 1968), https://obamawhitehouse.archives.gov/blog/2011/10/21/arc-moral-universe -long-it-bends-toward-justice.